OPPORTUNITIES

in

Property Management Careers

REVISED EDITION

MARIWYN EVANS

New York   Chicago   San Francisco   Lisbon   London   Madrid   Mexico City
Milan   New Delhi   San Juan   Seoul   Singapore   Sydney   Toronto

333.33

Library of Congress Cataloging-in-Publication Data

Evans, Mariwyn, 1949–
  Opportunities in property management careers / by Mariwyn Evans. — 3rd ed., rev.
    p.   cm.
  Includes bibliographical references.
  ISBN 0-07-148208-3 (alk. paper)
  1. Real estate management—Vocational guidance.   I. Title.

  HD1394.E93   2007
  647'.920683—dc22   2007010428

1 2 3 4 5 6 7 8 9 10 11 12 13 14 15 16 17 18 19   DOC/DOC   0 9 8 7

ISBN 978-0-07-148208-0
MHID   0-07-148208-3

Interior design by Rattray Design

McGraw-Hill books are available at special quantity discounts to use as premiums and sales promotions, or for use in corporate training programs. For more information, please write to the Director of Special Sales, Professional Publishing, McGraw-Hill, Two Penn Plaza, New York, NY 10121-2298. Or contact your local bookstore.

This book is printed on acid-free paper.

CONTENTS

Foreword   vii
Acknowledgments   ix

1. Property Managers Are Everywhere   1

Brief history of property management. Property
management today. Where property managers work.
Different property management jobs. Property
management as a career.

2. What Does a Property Manager Do?   17

Leasing and marketing. Overseeing financial
operations. Operating the property. Supervising
personnel. One title, many skills.

3. What Do Property Managers Manage?   35

Managing residential property. Managing office
buildings. Managing shopping centers. Managing
other types of property.

4. Entering the Property Management Field   45

Licensure. Education. Professional organizations.
Experience.

5. Factors Affecting Real Estate   57

Globalization of the real estate industry. Growth of
publicly owned real estate. Continuing flow of
capital. Consolidation of real estate. Changing
demographics. Strong economy, strong real estate
market.

6. On-Site Manager   67

Job description. Education. Earnings. Profile of an
apartment manager. Outlook.

7. Leasing Broker   73

Job description. Education. Earnings. Profile of a
leasing broker/property manager. Outlook.

8. Property Manager   81

Job description. Education. Earnings. Profile of a
property manager. Profile of a vice president of
property management. Outlook.

9. **Asset and Portfolio Manager** 93

   Job description. Education. Earnings. Profile of an
   asset manager. Profile of an REIT manager. Outlook.

10. **Property Manager as Business Owner** 103

    Demand for fee management. Starting a business.
    Earnings. Profile of an owner of a real estate
    business. Outlook.

11. **Careers Related to Property Management** 113

    Real estate sales. Property maintenance and systems
    administration. Clerical work. Other fields.

12. **Future of Property Management** 123

    Securitization of real estate. Technology and
    property management. Greening of commercial real
    estate. Offshoring and telecommuting. The future is
    bright.

Appendix A: Schools Offering Real Estate Majors 131
Appendix B: Associations 139
Additional Resources 143

FOREWORD

In May 2006, the news outlet CNN named property management one of the best jobs in America. This recognition reflects that fact that today, property management is a true profession. It requires sophisticated skills in accounting and financial reporting, a comprehensive understanding of state and federal regulations, and an ability to connect with and provide a high level of service to both owners and tenants.

The positive news for young people considering property management as a career is that the need for property management is increasing with every year that passes. As the population grows, more and more people rely on property managers to support their homes, businesses, restaurants, hotels, and factories. Investors have also acknowledged the importance of real estate and expect it to be managed at the highest levels.

Property management is both demanding and rewarding. It's also a career that allows for growth and advancement. For the individual who is service oriented, who cares about people, who can find solutions to tough problems, and who is excited by the prospect of a new challenge every day, property management holds the promise of a great future. This I can personally confirm from my own experience.

Robert Toothaker, CPM®
2007 President, Institute of Real Estate Management
Senior Executive Managing Director, CB Richard Ellis
South Bend, Indiana

Acknowledgments

I WOULD LIKE to thank the many property managers who are members of the Institute of Real Estate Management. Their professionalism and enthusiasm have taught me a great deal about what it takes to be a good property manager. I would also like to thank those property managers who took time from their schedules to be interviewed for this book.

1

PROPERTY MANAGERS ARE EVERYWHERE

MANY AMERICANS SPEND the majority of their lives in the suburbs living in single-family homes. If the roof needs to be fixed or the fence needs to be painted, the owner does the work or hires someone else to do it. In this world, there would seem to be no need for property managers.

Yet, even in the suburbs, property managers play a vital role. These real estate professionals are responsible for operating the malls and shopping centers that dot these localities. They manage and find tenants for the office parks and Main Streets where Americans work. They oversee the repairs and upkeep at condominiums and apartment buildings also located in the suburbs. And, of course, they manage the high-rise residences and offices in major urban areas.

Property managers have many jobs. They show property to prospective tenants and negotiate leases to rent apartments and other property. They also oversee the physical aspects of a property to make sure they operate smoothly. They or their employees do everything from repairing a faulty furnace to replacing a light bulb. They plan and supervise where walls should be placed inside office properties and how many security guards and parking places are needed at a mall. In addition, property managers often supervise major renovations of projects to make buildings more attractive and better able to serve the needs of tenants.

Property managers also are responsible for all the financial tasks associated with operating a large building. Managers develop yearly budgets of expenses and income to decide what rents they must charge to make a profit. Managers also oversee the spending at a property to make sure that expenses are in line with budgeted costs. Then they create reports for the building's owners on how much profit they can expect to receive on their investment. These reports may be a very simple one- or two-page summary or many pages of financial statements, depending on the size of the property and the wishes of the owners.

In many cases, property managers are also responsible for buying insurance for the properties to cover disasters and for paying property taxes and other charges owed to federal, state, and local governments. Another critical function of many property management jobs for larger buildings is supervising the maintenance, leasing, and accounting staffs.

Brief History of Property Management

Property management is a multifaceted job, with new and different challenges every day. However, property management did not start as such a responsible and complex endeavor. In its earliest days, the property manager had only one job—to collect the rent.

Rent Collectors

The idea of employing a person to collect payments for the use of property owned by another is perhaps as old as civilization. Even in the ancient worlds of Egypt, Greece, and Rome, the wealthy employed agents to collect payments from those who lived on and farmed their lands. As people began to live in cities, it became the rent collector's job to gather the rents from workers and merchants who occupied stores and apartments in parts of the city far from where the buildings' owners lived. These rent collectors, who were often feared and disliked, also found tenants for the few vacancies that occurred. For decades, collecting the rent remained the main job of the property manager.

The Depression and Property Managers

It was not until the Great Depression of the 1930s that events worked to transform the despised rent collector into the property manager we know today. The harsh economic conditions of the Depression made it difficult for many property owners to make mortgage and tax payments on their homes, stores, and office buildings. Unemployment was high, and many people were without work. Dust storms in the Southwest destroyed crops and left many farmers without income. During the same time, the stock market crash and the failure of numerous banks wiped out many people's savings.

Faced with these economic hardships, some property owners were unable to pay their mortgages or real estate taxes. As a result, banks and local governments were forced to take over the ownership of many homes and commercial buildings.

In general, when a bank takes over a property because of a mortgage default, it sells the property to another buyer. However, there were few people willing or able to buy during the Depression. As a result, the banks kept many of the properties.

Of course, the bankers did not have the time or knowledge to manage property, so they decided to hire others to collect the rent and look after these assets. Naturally, they looked for people who were honest, who knew what was needed to manage property, and who would make managing property a real business. Thus the property manager was born.

As individuals began to look at property management as a career, they organized professional groups to set standards of ethical conduct for property management professionals and to help assure banks that their members were trustworthy and experienced. Several property management organizations that are still in existence today began during the 1920s and 1930s, including the Building Owners and Managers Association (BOMA), the Institute of Real Estate Management (IREM), and the National Apartment Association (NAA).

Property Management Today

In the last several decades, the role of the property manager has changed dramatically. Even twenty-five years ago, most people became property managers by accident. It was not seen as a career in the same way that becoming a doctor or lawyer was. Today, however, real estate has become a major investment vehicle for pension funds, wealthy individuals, and even individual investors who own shares in companies that own and manage large properties. Because of the growth of real estate investment, the sophistication of the job continues to increase. In the twenty-first century, property management is indeed a full-time career.

The demand for property management and the salaries managers receive have grown tremendously in recent years. Surveys by the Institute of Real Estate Management revealed that compensation for managers has almost doubled in the last decade. Even better news for those entering the business is that salaries for beginning managers rise rapidly in the first five years of employment, reaching approximately half of the amount paid to experienced managers by that point. IREM says that in part this higher compensation is caused by a desire to attract younger people to the industry. Another factor is that owners expect managers to perform a wider range of functions than ever before.

Where Property Managers Work

Property managers are responsible for managing most of the larger office buildings, shopping centers, and apartment buildings in the United States today. According to *The Certified Property Manager Profile and Compensation Study*, a 2004 survey conducted by the Institute of Real Estate Management among its members, about 32 percent of those in property management work for a firm whose principal business is management. Another 36 percent work for full-service real estate companies that engage in selling real estate as well as managing it. Other types of employers include private owners (8 percent), investment or trust companies (7 percent), development companies (5 percent), financial institutions (2 percent), and government agencies (2 percent).

Third-Party Managers

Most property managers work directly for the owners of the properties they manage. These owners can be individuals, group investors who formed a partnership to buy a property, banks that hold properties in trusts, or corporations. Because they are paid a fee for their services (instead of a commission, as is usually the case for real estate brokers who sell property), these managers are sometimes called *fee managers*. As might be expected, the number of managers working for private owners—today most likely a pension fund, corporation, or real estate investment trust—has grown as these types of companies become more prominent in the commercial real estate industry.

Fee managers may be managing properties for many different owners at the same time. Some fee management companies specialize in one or two types of property, while others manage many types of property. The size of fee management companies also may vary widely, although more than half of fee management firms have twenty or fewer employees. Larger fee management firms may have regional offices that serve several states.

The 1990s was a decade of significant consolidation among real estate management firms, as was the case with many other types of service industries. Many local and regional firms merged to gain economies of scale that would enable them to compete nationally and, in some cases, globally. These firms offer not only property management service but development, corporate management, and brokerage services as well. They believe, and many experts share their view, that clients want the efficiencies that such one-stop shopping can provide. Some of these national and international companies also own considerable amounts of real estate, which they manage on their own behalf.

While many experts expect consolidation to continue in the real estate industry, the strong commercial real estate markets of the 2000s have also prompted the formation of many small, local "boutique" firms that specialize in personal service and experience in one market. Real estate remains primarily a local industry; even the largest national firms command no more than a single-digit percentage share of the commercial market.

Although 54 percent of property managers responding to the 2004 IREM survey still worked for property management firms employing fifty or fewer people, smaller independent fee management companies may be losing ground to larger national fee management companies and to institutional real estate operations. In the same survey, 21 percent of respondents worked for companies with more than two hundred employees.

Many property managers may aspire to own their own companies, but working for a fee management company or the property management department of a full-service real estate company has many advantages. For those with little experience in management, the fee management company may be more willing to consider hiring inexperienced managers for a first job. In addition, because the success of the fee management business depends on how well it can perform, fee managers are more likely to be judged on their skills than on whether they have a college degree, although this is less true than it was a decade ago, especially at large, national companies. Successful management companies generally give employees opportunities for rapid advancement if they perform well. Working for a fee management company also gives an employee the opportunity to learn how a fee management business is operated, with the idea of perhaps starting his or her own business some day.

There may also be some drawbacks to working for a fee management company. Because the income of the management company or department depends on the number of properties it has under management contract at any one time, losing a large management account may necessitate laying off employees. Thus, a job with a fee manager may be less secure than one with a large corporation or with a real estate investment trust, which is more likely to have the resources to survive temporary setbacks. And in small fee management companies, there may not be as much room for advancement after an employee reaches a certain level.

According to the 2004 IREM survey, members working for fee management companies averaged annual compensation of $91,000, which includes both U.S.-based managers and Canadian members associated with IREM through The Real Estate Institute of Canada. Those managers working for full-service real estate companies averaged $97,500. Statistics Canada calculated that real estate rental and leasing agents, a group that includes some managers, averaged an hourly rate of $16.05 (Canadian dollars) in 2005.

Real Estate Investment Trusts

Another source of employment for real estate managers are real estate investment trusts (REITs). Congress created REITs during the 1960s as a means for small investors to participate in real estate. However, in was not until the 1990s that REITs assumed an important place in the real estate investment industry. In Canada, REIT structures were not legalized until 1993. Today, REITs are also in many countries in Europe and Asia and are a major factor in financing real estate. In 2006, the National Association of Real Estate Investment Trusts estimated that about $330,691,000 were invested in U.S. REITs. During the early 1990s, real estate owners faced severe shortages of financing from banks and other typical real estate lenders. Because real estate traditionally has been financed through loans, many developers were unable to do business and even faced bankruptcy. In an effort to find new ways to fund their businesses, many turned to REITs.

Simply, an REIT is a company dedicated to owning and managing income-producing real estate. Some also engage in financing real estate. A unique feature of REITs is that they must by law pay out 95 percent of their taxable income to stockholders. To have money for operations, REITs issue stock on the public stock market. It is this ability to acquire capital from the stock market, rather than from banks and other lenders, that made REITs so attractive to private real estate companies in the 1990s. In 2006 there were some 185 REITs, although analysts predict that some of these companies may merge in the decade ahead. Some REITs have also bought up public shares and returned to private ownership in recent years. This trend has been more pronounced lately, and many experts expect it to continue as long as interest rates are low. REITs own approximately $475 billion of investment real estate, and these assets all need property managers.

Property managers who oversee properties for REITs generally are employees of the company rather than third-party managers. Many REITs are national with regional offices in a number of cities; others specialize in one geographic area. Most REITs specialize in one property type, such as offices, apartments, and so forth.

Many of the responsibilities of REIT property managers are similar to those of their third-party counterparts. However, REITs also must be concerned with satisfying the demands of stockholders and real estate market analysts, whose opinions may affect the price of their stock.

On the positive side, REITs, like large national real estate companies, usually are able to offer a wider range of benefits and more chances for advancement than smaller firms. Also, because they are public companies, many REITs can offer employees stock options. The 2004 IREM survey found that managers working for a trust or investment company earned total compensation of $113,000.

Institutional Owners

Pension funds, banks, large limited partnerships of individuals who do not know each other, and even foreign investors make up another sizable group of building owners that requires the services of property managers. Collectively, this group is sometimes referred to as *institutional owners.*

Although many of these groups still hire independent fee managers, some larger owners hire property managers who work directly for their companies. These employees perform many of the same jobs as a fee manager, but they often manage only property owned by their employers. However, some institutional owners are also competing for fee management contracts, so some institutional employees may also be engaged in fee management.

Institutional owners were not very active during the 1990s, but in recent years, the attraction of real estate as a stable source of regular cash flow has become more attractive to pension funds and prompted them to purchase more real estate. Likewise, many foreign investors are beginning to return to U.S. commercial real estate markets, aided by the weaker dollar. These owners, too, depend upon the skills of property managers to operate their assets.

The 2004 IREM survey found that its members who worked for financial institutions earned an average annual salary of $95,500.

Corporate Real Estate Management

While much of this book focuses on the management of income-producing real estate that is owned by private investors, another larger segment of real estate that requires property management is owned by corporations. Corporations own more than half of all investment real estate (which excludes owner-occupied housing). Properties owned by corporations range from factories and warehouses to corporate office facilities and even occasionally corporate housing. Large nonprofit entities such as hospitals, universities, and airports also use the services of facilities managers. In 2006, approximately seventy-five hundred individuals were members of CoreNet Global, the country's largest association for corporate real estate. These individuals work directly for corporations and oversee all aspects of a company's real estate needs, from development to management to sales. Some undertake management of corporate facilities in-house, although in recent years more and more companies have outsourced some or all of the facilities management functions to specialized facilities management companies or to the facilities divisions of large national real estate service firms. Many experts believe that the trend toward outsourcing will continue.

Corporate real estate executives perform or oversee many management functions. In addition, corporate managers are often responsible for ensuring that a company's employees have the facilities they need to meet corporate goals. As a result, corporate managers often participate in strategic planning initiatives to predict future real estate needs. They also may be responsible for obtaining furniture systems and building fixtures, for operating building facilities such as mail rooms, and for leasing or developing needed real estate space.

Salaries for corporate real estate executives are higher than are those for third-party managers. A CoreNet Global member survey in 2003 revealed that the average salary for the top real estate officer was $227,727; the average salary for a chief facilities management officer was $162,476. The 2004 IREM survey found that those in corporate positions averaged $97,500 in compensation. The majority of the compensation came from base salaries or bonuses; little came from commissions. In addition, because they are employees of large corporations, corporate real estate executives enjoy the benefits and stock-option plans offered to all corporate employees.

Different Property Management Jobs

Many property managers perform tasks at more than one level, so it's often helpful to divide the management function into five different jobs.

- On-site manager
- Leasing agent
- Tenant representative
- Property manager
- Portfolio manager

On-Site Manager

The on-site, or resident, manager is a property manager responsible for the day-to-day operation of one property. The on-site manager is often the entry-level job in property management. The on-site manager may sometimes live at the apartment complex he or she manages, and most office buildings and shopping centers also have site managers on the premises.

The on-site manager has the most daily contact with tenants and performs most of the routine tasks of management, such as collecting rent, preparing reports, and supervising maintenance and cleaning workers.

Leasing Agent

The leasing agent, or leasing broker, is responsible for locating and signing new tenants to occupy space in a building. This job is sales oriented and is not concerned with the daily operations of the property, except as they affect the leasing effort.

A leasing agent may work exclusively for one property, especially if it is large, or he or she may be transferred from one property to another as each property becomes fully leased. A leasing agent working at a small office or apartment complex may be relatively inexperienced and may report to the property manager or the on-site manager. On the other hand, a leasing agent for a larger office complex may have years of sales experience and report directly to the portfolio manager. However, not all properties employ separate leasing agents. In these cases, the on-site manager and/or the property supervisor handle the leasing duties.

Tenant Representative

A variation on the job of leasing broker is that of tenant representative, who performs many of the functions of a leasing broker but works on behalf of the prospective tenant instead of the owner. Most tenant representatives work in commercial property and rarely in the apartment area. Tenant representatives assist prospective tenants in locating space, analyzing how well the space and the building fit the prospect's needs, and working as part of a team to negotiate lease and interior construction terms.

Property Manager

The property manager, sometimes called the real estate manager, is usually responsible for the operation of several properties. The property manager typically makes frequent visits to each property to evaluate the property's performance. He or she also oversees the work of the on-site manager for each property.

In addition, the property manager is usually a participant in planning management policies and budgets for the properties under his or her supervision. This manager usually takes first-line responsibility for seeing that space is leased and that expenses are in line with the budget. Depending on the size of the company, the property manager may also meet directly with property owners to discuss the status of a given property. Property managers usually report to an asset manager.

Asset Manager

The asset, or portfolio, manager is an executive responsible for a large number of properties and, in many cases, for the operation of the real estate company or department. Although this manager may visit individual properties, he or she relies on financial information and reports from property managers to evaluate the performance of each property.

The asset manager acts as a substitute for a property's owner or owners. He or she approves long-range plans for properties, sets general management policies, and approves the largest financial expenditures. The asset manager may also advise owners on the best time to buy, sell, or renovate a particular property.

In many instances, the asset manager may also be responsible for generating new business for the fee management company or the real estate department. This job involves presentations to owners and corporate owners as well as frequent travel. The asset manager represents the top of the property management pyramid. Property management is still a field that offers many chances to climb up that pyramid.

Property Management as a Career

Investment real estate represents perhaps the single largest source of wealth in this country. For example, in the first half of 2006, more than $290 billion was invested in U.S. real estate, according to the global consulting firm Jones Lang LaSalle. The owners of this real estate—whether they are individuals or large institutions— recognize that to protect this investment and make profits from it, they need the services of skilled real estate management professionals. They rely on these individuals to build a property's value by leasing it at the highest possible rates. They expect managers to preserve a building's value by maintaining it well. Finally, they look to property managers to help improve a building's value through renovation. All of these needs help ensure that property managers will be in great demand in the years ahead.

2

What Does a Property Manager Do?

As Chapter 1 described, the simplest way to understand what property managers do is to think about them as the caretakers of buildings. However, this simple definition only scratches the surface of the dozens of job responsibilities that the average property manager must handle.

A manager's specific job tasks will vary based on both the type—residential, office, retail—and the size of a property. However, a property manager also may be responsible for:

- Creating promotional materials for properties
- Showing vacant space to prospective tenants
- Negotiating leases with tenants and their attorneys

- Keeping in contact with current tenants to ensure that they are happy with the property
- Hiring and supervising a staff that may include other property managers and maintenance personnel
- Working with vendors to acquire the goods and services a property needs to operate
- Developing a budget estimating possible income and expenses
- Keeping financial records for rent collected and money spent
- Analyzing competing properties to better understand the best way to market the property
- Working with lawyers to evict tenants who do not pay their rent or who violate other requirements of their leases
- Getting bids for and purchasing insurance, environmental consulting, security, and other services needed for building operations
- Advising the owner when major repairs or renovations of the property are needed
- Assisting the owner in deciding when to sell the property

As this list demonstrates, a property manager's job is varied and requires many different types of skills. In a larger company, a property manager may specialize in only one type of job, such as supervising personnel. In a smaller firm, a manager may do many, if not all, the jobs listed above.

To understand more about the complex job of property management, it is useful to break down the tasks into four broad categories: leasing and marketing, overseeing financial operations, operating the property, and supervising personnel.

Leasing and Marketing

Finding tenants for a property is perhaps the single most critical function that a property manager performs. Without tenants, there is no income for the owner or salary for the manager. Leasing activities involve locating tenants for a property, showing available space at the property to prospective tenants, and negotiating leases for space with new and existing tenants.

Finding suitable tenants for a property is an important part of the property manager's responsibilities. Leasing is especially important today, because many cities have an oversupply of office buildings, shopping centers, and apartments for rent. In such cases, an effective leasing campaign is vital to the success of the property.

Market Research

Today, finding tenants, especially for larger properties, involves a lot more than just putting a sign out front. The first step in locating tenants is determining which companies or individuals might be most interested in the property. Property managers coordinating larger, more expensive projects often spend many thousands of dollars researching the market for the property. They will use market research specialists to review census data on income, population, and other factors affecting markets. Today, a large amount of property data are available over the Internet, although not always free of charge. Researchers will present the data to a property management leasing team, which will then develop a marketing plan for the property.

At smaller properties and in less-populated areas, market research may be less formal. A manager may survey current tenants to see what they are like and what appeals to them about the property. These data will help determine the kinds of people or businesses that are already interested in the property. Managers also may visit similar properties to see how the competition is marketing its product. The market research aspect of leasing is becoming much more important because of the increased competition for tenants. A job in market research with a larger company is a good stepping-stone to a career in leasing.

Whether property managers perform research themselves or analyze data from other sources, effective market research requires the ability to understand the meaning of many diverse pieces of information and how these pieces fit together. Analytical skills are an essential part of understanding the market. A good understanding of people and the psychology of buying is also important to developing a plan for marketing property.

Unless a property is very small, at least part of the market analysis and planning is handled by sales and leasing specialists who work for the management firm. However, the site manager and the supervising property manager should participate in this planning because they have a closer contact with the property and its current residents.

Once a marketing plan has been developed for a property, the manager uses advertising, special events at the property, and other efforts to let the target market know about the property. If the advertising is successful, the property manager will begin the second part of the leasing job—showing vacant space to prospects.

Showing the Space

Like market research, leasing activities may be handled by leasing specialists or performed by the on-site property manager. Generally, leasing specialists are used for larger office, industrial, or shopping center properties, where tenants may come from all parts of the region or even from across the country. New buildings are also more likely to rely on leasing brokers. At apartment buildings and small office and shopping centers, the leasing is more likely to be done by the property management staff responsible for overseeing the building's operations.

Regardless of who shows a space, certain sales skills are involved in leasing. Before showing an apartment or commercial space to a prospect, the leasing agent needs to determine whether the prospect is qualified. Personal questions and a credit and reference check will determine whether the prospect is financially able to afford the space. Asking personal questions to assess needs and financial worthiness is called *qualifying the prospect.*

Personal questions will also help the leasing agent determine which of the available spaces would be best suited to the needs and desires of the tenant. For example, faced with two prospects who are interested in renting a one-bedroom apartment, careful questions by the leasing agent may reveal that one person wants quiet to study while another wants plentiful light for a large plant collection. By showing each an apartment that meets these special needs, the leasing agent helps ensure that these prospects are satisfied.

Asking questions that reveal this information while keeping the prospect pleasantly interested requires good verbal skills and an understanding of human psychology. Often people are offended by point-blank questions such as, "Have neighbors complained about your stereo?" Naturally, this type of information must be gathered subtly. Likewise, a tenant may have a desire that is not at first apparent but that is an important key in leasing the apartment successfully. For example, the person looking for a quiet apartment may really be concerned about safety rather than noise. By listening carefully to what is said and asking insightful follow-up questions, the leasing agent may uncover what the prospect's real concerns are.

Negotiating Leases

The final task of the leasing agent is to negotiate the lease. Negotiation involves give-and-take between the leasing agent and the tenant, and usually the attorneys for both parties. The goal of each party is to get the best terms and the most reasonable rent. The property manager has the extra burden of ensuring that both the owner and the tenant are satisfied with the lease terms, so that once installed, the tenant will be content with the property.

In an apartment rental, a standard-form lease may be used. In such instances, the leasing agent should understand the provisions of the lease and be able to explain them to the tenant. However, little real negotiation is likely to go on. Perhaps the tenant may want the apartment painted or want to move in one day sooner, but these minor concessions will usually be made by the leasing agent. And because most apartment leases last for only one year, changes in terms and rental rates are usually negotiated only when a new lease is signed.

Lease negotiation for office space, retail stores, or industrial property is usually a more complicated affair. While there are some standard provisions that are often included in commercial leases, each lease is negotiated separately.

Commercial and industrial leases usually run for a much longer period than do apartment leases, perhaps five to seven years. Therefore, changes in the rental rate over the period of the lease have to be negotiated when the initial lease is signed.

Commercial leases also involve other charges besides rent, such as heat, cost of maintaining lobbies and halls, and tax and insurance costs. The final decision on who will pay for all of these costs is usually negotiated. Similarly, who will pay for the costs of decorating the space, putting in lights, and painting walls is subject to negotiation in commercial leases.

Because of the complexity involved in commercial lease negotiation, lawyers often participate in all or part of the negotiation. However, the give-and-take in establishing the terms of the agreement is still carried out by leasing specialists.

The complex issues involved in negotiations require a good understanding of the legal meaning of lease clauses. Negotiators must also know the financial impact of various lease concessions so that they will secure the best terms for the owners. Finally, negotiators must have a vast understanding of human psychology to react to the negotiating strategies of the other party. This combination of salesmanship, psychology, and analytical skills is key to success in the important management area of marketing and leasing.

Leasing and Marketing on the Internet

As is the case with many aspects of society, the Internet and the World Wide Web have had an impact on the real estate industry. Commercial real estate companies now have their own sites, and most provide specific information about space available for rent. A variety of websites specializing in showing available apartments and commercial space also have become much more widely used. However, unlike residential real estate, there are no centralized listing databases for commercial properties. For example, sites such as LoopNet (www.loopnet.com) and Co-Star (www.costar.com) offer properties in all parts of the United States and Canada, but their content by no means constitutes all commercial properties for sale or lease. The Commercial Council of the Canadian Real Estate

Association also maintains a property listing site (www.icx.ca). As a result, prospective buyers and tenants often must rely on a local agent for assistance in locating properties.

Managers of multifamily properties now rely extensively on certain Internet sites such as Craigslist (craigslist.com) and RentNet (www.rent net.com) to lease apartments. These sites not only permit interested parties to check availabilities and prices, look at floor plans, and get directions to the property, some even offer a virtual tour, which enables prospects to "walk through" an apartment and view rooms and property features from different angles. Many properties under construction position cameras so that prospects can follow the construction in real time. Still other sites specialize in demographic or market information that is vital in making leasing or construction decisions for offices, factories, and shopping malls.

Managers also increasingly use the Internet as a way for tenants to communicate their needs. Management company websites often enable tenants to make maintenance requests, check on building functions and activities, and even pay the rent online.

Although the complexity of commercial transactions and the lack of consistent definitions of commercial property terminology make it less likely that a complete leasing or sales transaction will be completed remotely, industry groups are now working toward standards that will allow for detailed transfer of property information and contracts more easily.

Overseeing Financial Operations

Analytical skills are also an essential part of the second major area in which the property manager works—financial record keeping and budgeting. Although successful leasing is vital to a building's initial success, good financial management ensures the property's success.

Record Keeping

Managing a building involves a tremendous amount of record keeping. Rent payments and other income must be received and documented. If rents are late or not paid, tenants must receive notices and, if necessary, eviction procedures must begin.

Bills must be paid to staff, suppliers of the many products needed for building operation, and outside contractors. Taxes, insurance, and other costs must be kept up to date. Contracts for supplies and services must be negotiated. All of this record keeping is made much more complex because the property management company oversees the operations of many buildings. Income from each building must be recorded separately and not mixed with other funds. And because most buildings have several owners, each must receive the proper amount of profits and the correct information about his or her property.

Expenses for repairs, staff, and services also must be divided among the buildings that require the service. For example, a management company may have a contract with a landscaping firm to care for the lawns at all the office buildings it manages. However, a share of the overall costs and any special expenses must be charged to the individual building owners. If the property manager is also the owner of the management company or the supervisor of a management department, he or she may have to take responsibility for office supply and personnel budgets.

Although much of the actual record keeping may be handled by bookkeepers or clerical personnel, the property manager must keep an accurate, detailed account of all income and expenses. While an accounting degree is not essential, the manager must have a good basic grasp of how financial reports are created and interpreted. Knowledge of basic programs such as spreadsheets and presentation software is critical; knowledge of specialized property management programs for analysis is desirable.

As property management has become more sophisticated, asset and portfolio managers who oversee many larger properties and securities analysts who evaluate the performance of real estate investment trusts rely on financial reports to give them immediate information on how well a property is performing. These high-level managers review regular reports on earnings, expenses, and taxes and use them to analyze a building's profitability. Asset managers and analysts also compare a building's financial performance with similar properties to determine if the manager is doing a good job and if the building should be improved or sold.

For those who want to move into the role of asset manager, a broad understanding of finance is essential. Some asset managers hold advanced business degrees or come into real estate from banking or other financial positions.

Budgeting

Another financial function that is closely related to financial analysis is budgeting. Developing an annual budget for a property is one of the most important parts of the property manager's job. Budgeting must be based on both past experience and anticipated future performance.

In comparing a property's past performance against the budget, a property or asset manager must determine why certain expenses are higher (was it a one-time problem or an ongoing one?) and whether these expenses need to be raised in the coming year. Managers should also contact suppliers of products and discuss whether prices will increase in the coming year. In this way, budget projections will be more accurate. Budgets also should include planned costs for major and minor repairs for the coming year. Finally, each category of expense should be reviewed to find ways to reduce costs.

After comparing expenses and projecting the next year's costs, the budgeting process must consider how closely income projections are being met. Income for a building comes primarily from rents, so the first consideration is whether leasing efforts have kept the property full. Analysis also must determine if rents being charged are reasonable and competitive with similar buildings. If planned rental income is not being met, new budgeting should include plans for improving leasing. Perhaps money will be added to the expense budget for additional advertising.

Other income also will be included in the budget. The manager should consider how income from vending machines and laundry rooms, parking fees, and other sources can be increased. A combination of increased income and reduced expenses will yield income for the property owner and ensure satisfaction with the property manager's performance.

A manager's involvement in the budgeting process depends on the size of the company and his or her expertise. Rarely does an on-site manager have total responsibility for a property budget. However, both the on-site manager and the maintenance personnel contribute to the final product. In a national company, budgets for some items may be consolidated on a regional level. Budgets for a property are generally approved by the owner and/or portfolio manager involved in the project. A well-prepared budget is the tool the property manager uses to operate the property and the asset manager uses to determine how well the property is being operated.

Operating the Property

Much of the day-to-day work of the property manager can be classified as operating the property. Operations include collecting rent, notifying residents of new rules and procedures at the property, maintaining contact with residents to ensure their satisfaction, purchasing supplies and services, ensuring that all parts of the property are well maintained, and seeing that any problems are resolved. Depending on the day, operations may be as simple as walking through the property and greeting residents or as complex as coordinating evacuation for a bomb scare. It is often said that there is no such thing as a routine day in property management.

Tenant Relations

As many types of property have become overbuilt, maintaining good relations with tenants and keeping them at the property have become increasingly important aspects of the property manager's job. Tenant relations fall into two categories: ongoing relations and problem solving. Like leasing, both aspects of tenant relations require a good understanding of human psychology and the ability to listen.

Ongoing Relations

At its simplest, good ongoing tenant relations require that the manager like the tenants and the tenants like the manager. Good tenant relations occur when the manager and all the building staff seem available, polite, concerned, and involved. Programs that help to build good tenant relations include:

• **A tenant newsletter.** This is a good vehicle for informing tenants about problems, rule changes, and other news as well as for building a sense of community with tenants. Some properties have websites to share tenant news, or they send regular e-newletters to tenants. Other options include building intranets.

• **Tenant events.** Holiday parties, lunchtime speakers, or trips all gain points with tenants.

• **Organizing needed services.** A day-care center, transportation to shopping for elderly residents, and security escorts to the parking lot can give tenants a sense that management cares about their concerns and needs.

• **Regular visits with tenants.** Establishing a relationship that extends beyond just solving problems helps when problems do arise.

Good tenant relations require genuine concern for others and a friendly, outgoing manner. A good understanding of tenant needs and good organizational skills also help.

Problem Solving

The other, less-enjoyable part of tenant relations is handling complaints. However, if overall tenant relations are good, problems will be easier to solve. One key to effectively handling complaints is giving tenants someone to talk with about their problem. A manager or maintenance worker should be on call day and night to answer emergencies. A voice mail account also should be set up to take nonemergency calls. For maintenance complaints, scheduling should allow for quick response.

Another key to answering complaints effectively is to listen and communicate. The manager must be certain to listen carefully and understand what the real complaint is. Keeping the lines of communication open and getting back to tenants with an answer as soon as possible cools tempers and assures tenants of management concern. Finally, the manager should contact the tenant after the problem is solved to reassure the tenant and find out if the complaint could be handled better in the future.

Tact, patience, and honesty go a long way in making problem solving effective. Good communications skills also ensure that complaints do not grow out of proportion.

Maintenance and Janitorial Tasks

Maintaining the physical appearance and safety of a property is one of the most basic yet vital tasks of the property manager. Maintenance involves both repairing broken equipment and developing a long-term plan for taking care of equipment so that it will remain in good working order. Although property managers or on-site managers seldom perform maintenance themselves, planning maintenance activities is part of the operations job. In addition, managers may oversee the work of maintenance and janitorial personnel at properties that do not have a full-time maintenance supervisor.

Because of the large number of components that make up a building, maintenance of the building is a continual task. Routine tasks include cleaning furnaces and air conditioners, cleaning swimming pools, painting, plumbing, general cleaning and removing trash, removing leaves and exterior debris, paving and repairing parking lots, repairing roofs, cleaning carpets and floors, washing windows, and changing light bulbs. Maintenance workers may also perform work for individual tenants, including hanging pictures, installing special lighting, and moving furniture.

Depending on how often each task needs to be done, the property manager will create an annual maintenance schedule of work. In this way, all jobs are done when necessary and are not overlooked. At the same time, a complete schedule ensures that maintenance workers use their time well. Of course, any well-planned schedule should allow time for emergencies.

In addition to work performed by in-house maintenance staff, most properties use various contractors to perform special maintenance tasks. In some cases, these outside vendors are called in to perform a special repair, such as installing a new roof or a new floor in the lobby. In other cases, the manager may decide that it is more economical to hire an outside service to perform a specific job, such as lawn care or elevator maintenance. Ongoing maintenance work is usually done under a contract that is negotiated by the property manager.

Effective maintenance work is based on attention to detail and careful planning. A manager must have both a good understanding of the tasks involved and the ability to follow through and ensure that the job is done correctly. Because much maintenance work is done by other employees, the property manager must also call on personnel supervisory skills to implement an effective maintenance program.

Purchasing

Negotiating contracts with suppliers of maintenance services is just one aspect of the purchasing involved with a property. In selecting outside maintenance suppliers, the on-site or property manager usually writes a detailed explanation of the job involved and then asks several possible vendors to give cost estimates—or bids—on the work. The manager must check references and compare prices and quality of work. Once the work is done, the manager should evaluate it to be sure that it has been done correctly.

Effective vendor negotiation requires that the manager have a good understanding of the job involved; otherwise, it would be difficult to determine if it has been done well. Financial and negotiating skills are also important in arriving at a good final contract.

Evaluating both the quality and price of products used in the management of a property is also part of the property manager's job. Paper products, paint, carpeting and draperies, cleaning supplies, and light bulbs are just a few of the items managers buy regularly. Depending on the organization and the size of the property, purchasing may be centralized for several properties or handled by the site manager or maintenance supervisor. In some cases, purchasing is centralized through purchasing agents at national companies or by using third-party national buying groups to lower costs.

As is the case with vendor contracts, the manager must explore alternatives, check references, and compare quality and price before making a final decision. Because of the tremendous importance of controlling costs in property operations, effective purchasing can make a major contribution to the overall success of the property.

Supervising Personnel

Because of the large number of people needed to manage most buildings, personnel supervision is a part of almost every manager's job, from the on-site to the asset manager. The combination of people and detail-oriented skills needed to do all the jobs involved in property management adds another level of difficulty to the hiring and supervision of management personnel. In hiring, the property manager must be particularly aware of the orientation of each job and hire accordingly. People skills are less important than accuracy if handling rental receipts is an important part of the job. On the other hand, a leasing agent should be chosen primarily because of his or her selling skills.

Many of the hiring and supervision practices of property management are the same as those used in any other business. However, there are a few considerations to keep in mind.

Because the role of the property management staff is to serve the needs of the tenants and to handle all problems that arise, management employees must be willing to work long hours if needed and put the concerns of tenants before their own needs. For an on-site manager living at a property, the job may truly seem to be a twenty-four-hour one.

Higher-level property and portfolio management jobs may also require a great deal of travel, and this element should be made clear in hiring and training personnel. National companies may have scattered properties that require site visits and regular inspections. Even local companies usually have properties located throughout a city.

One Title, Many Skills

As you can see, to succeed, property managers must have a wide range of skills—from finance to legal issues and from working with people to setting up and managing complex computerized systems. Tasks such as lease negotiation and tenant relations require good people skills and an outgoing personality. Financial record keeping and market analysis require a factual, detail-oriented mind. Supervising personnel and purchasing require a little of each of these skills.

It is the rare property manager who performs all of the tasks described in this chapter—particularly today, when there is an increasing trend toward specialization in the industry. Nonetheless, the property manager must still be a generalist who is good at many things. That, for many, is the hardest and the most exciting part of property management.

3

What Do Property Managers Manage?

MANY OF THE functions of property managers remain the same regardless of the type of property they manage. Whatever the building, managers have to lease space, create and oversee budgets, maintain the physical property, and supervise a staff. However, each major property type—apartment building, office building, shopping center, and industrial property—has its own special requirements and demands. For this reason, most property managers specialize in the management of one principal type of property. In smaller cities, some managers may manage all major property types successfully, but this has become less and less common as property management has become more sophisticated. Of course, many managers may decide to change from one property type to another during the course of a career.

Managing Residential Property

Many property managers begin their careers managing apartment buildings. Several factors contribute to this trend. Apartment properties are often smaller, leases are simpler and last for a shorter period than office or retail agreements, and the financial record keeping is less complex. For all these reasons, apartment management makes a good entree to property management. At the same time, property supervisors and asset managers working with residential properties often earn salaries roughly equal to managers of other property types, and they also have as much management expertise and experience.

Residential management focuses on three principal types of multifamily housing: conventionally financed rental apartments, federally assisted housing, and condominiums and cooperatives.

Other types of residential property, including rented single-family homes, mobile homes, college and university housing, and resort properties, may also require the services of a property manager. Although management is similar for these three types, there are some variations.

Conventionally Financed Apartments

The majority of apartment buildings fall into the conventionally financed category. *Conventionally financed* means that money to buy or build the apartment building was borrowed from a standard bank or other financing source. These apartment buildings are called conventionally financed to differentiate them from federally assisted apartment buildings, which receive part of their operating or mortgage money from one or more federal programs. However, most of the tasks involved in conventional apartment management also apply to federally assisted buildings. (Residential properties owned by real estate investment trusts are operated much the same as conventional apartment buildings, so they will not be discussed as a separate category.)

Most rental apartments come under the heading of conventionally financed. In a 2004 IREM survey, results showed that slightly more than 39 percent of those property managers surveyed managed conventionally financed apartments.

Managers of conventional residential rentals often devote a great deal of their time to leasing. Although each negotiation may be simpler than that for a commercial building, the volume is often higher. Unlike commercial properties, most apartment leases run for one year or less, so managers must constantly keep track of leases up for renewal and work with current tenants to get new leases signed.

In addition, residential managers must regularly show vacant apartments to prospects, especially during summer months when the majority of rentals occur. This schedule may require more night and weekend work than would be found at an office building site.

Residential property managers are also much more likely to be involved with the lives of their tenants than are commercial managers. Because of the emotions associated with the idea of home, residential tenants are often more demanding of repairs and security issues than are commercial tenants. Tenant reactions and complaints about property operations and the activities of other tenants often are more strongly felt and expressed in a residential setting.

The residential property manager probably devotes more time and effort to resident social events than do commercial managers. Apartment properties are more likely to sponsor parties and other tenant events than are office properties. Although these events may be fun, they are extra work for the residential manager.

Financial record keeping for conventionally financed apartments often involves a great deal of computer work in recording monthly rent payments and late payment fees. Managers of these properties are also more concerned with the possibility that tenants might disappear into the night without paying their rent than are managers of commercial properties. Residential properties often require security deposits, which must be carefully administered in a separate trust account, according to state law.

Federally Assisted Housing

As the cost of housing rises, some Americans—low-income workers and the elderly in particular—turn to the federal government for help in affording a decent place to live. Federally assisted housing requires the manager to handle more complex financial and tenant record keeping than does conventional apartment management. To qualify for government payments on mortgages and rent, managers of federally assisted properties must often file specific forms to show that the property and its tenants qualify for this assistance. (Other types of residential properties that rely on government assistance, such as low-income tax-credit housing, operate in much the same way as federally assisted housing and thus will not be discussed separately.)

Specifics of this required reporting differ with the type of government program involved. Some common reports include a requalification to demonstrate that the tenant's income is low enough to qualify for assistance and a form applying for payment of authorized subsidies. Completing all of this paperwork correctly and on time requires more attention to detail than may be needed in conventional apartment management. Knowledge of specialized software for assisted-housing management is also highly desirable.

Tenant relations is also an important part of managing federally assisted housing. Because many tenants are poor, elderly, or unemployed, they may need more service support from the property manager. Special education programs, day care for single mothers, transportation for the elderly, and other needed services often may be initiated and administered by the property manager. The manager also must show creativity in finding sources of staffing and funding for these programs and services, because few federally assisted properties have their own resources for such activities.

According to the 2004 IREM survey, almost 13 percent of those responding managed at least some federally assisted property. Another 2 percent managed publicly owned housing leased to low-income tenants. Compensation for this type of management is somewhat lower than that for conventional apartments.

Condominiums and Cooperatives

In larger cities and increasingly in smaller towns, home buyers are purchasing condominiums and townhomes instead of stand-alone homes. Condominiums are often less expensive, an important consideration for first-time buyers. Older people also find condominiums appealing because they generally do not have responsibility for upkeep of the physical property and shared land areas. Instead, this maintenance is the responsibility of a property manager.

Except for the fact that very little leasing activity is usually involved, operating a condominium complex is very much like conventional apartment management. The exception is the responsibility of the property manager to meet with the condominium's board of directors.

The board of directors is made up of individual owners who are elected by all the owners and who are entrusted to make operating decisions. This board works with the manager to develop budgets, decide on repairs, and buy services. However, because many condominium board members have little real estate experience, the property manager may find that they make unreasonable demands or refuse to spend funds on needed repairs. Working effectively with a condominium board is probably the most difficult aspect of this type of management.

The 2004 IREM survey found that 11 percent of those responding managed some condominium properties. However, compensation for condominium managers is the lowest of any management category surveyed. Indeed, it is often the case that condominium management is assigned to the least experienced member of the property management company.

Managing Office Buildings

Office building management requires many of the same skills as residential management, as well as a few more. Property managers who specialize in office building management are typically responsible for the smooth operation of properties that total many thousands of square feet and that often have highly sophisticated requirements for building equipment and security.

Leasing and financial management of an office building is generally more complex than that for apartment space. Office building leases usually last for several years, and the terms are worked out between attorneys and management. Office leases also include many other charges, such as the cost of maintaining lobbies and halls and charges for maintenance. All of these provisions must be negotiated as part of a lease. In addition, the property manager must keep track of the many building charges paid for by tenants and provide careful records of costs when tenants are billed.

In some cases, office building leasing is also performed by the property manager. But generally today, a special leasing broker is hired to locate tenants for vacant office space. Leasing an office building often demands more sophisticated advertising and research than is done for apartments. If the property manager is responsible for leasing space, he or she must maintain extensive records on businesses in the area that would be suited to the building and stay in touch with such business owners.

Although maintenance and tenant relations are important to the office building tenants, the focus is somewhat different. The business tenants who occupy rented office space depend on usable space with no maintenance problems so that they can do business efficiently. For this reason, pressure to perform routine maintenance and repairs promptly is even more important in the office building.

Because the lobby and/or grounds of an office building affect the reactions of those coming to do business there, the appearance of these areas requires constant maintenance, day and night. Nightly cleaning crews hired by the property manager also must be supervised.

Many office buildings or corporate facilities also offer ancillary services—from restaurants to day-care and exercise facilities—that must be overseen by the property manager. In some cases, the services at these facilities are supplied by third parties, but the manager must be certain that contract terms are met, that the property is adequately maintained, and that the tenants are satisfied with the services.

Tenant relations have a slightly different focus in office building management. Because leasing decisions are usually made by business owners or office managers in an office setting, the property manager concentrates more of his or her time in maintaining contact with the important decision makers. In part, this contact is social, as it is in an apartment building. Property managers may plan tenant events, such as lectures on interesting topics, picnics, concerts, and athletic competitions, during lunches and after work. Such events create goodwill and keep tenants happy with the property.

However, because these tenants are businesses interested in improving their profitability, a part of the office building manager's job is to assist them in lowering costs for lights, heat, and other charges. Managers also play a role in ensuring that business owners have what they need to operate—special electrical outlets and air-conditioning for computer equipment, and convenient services such as express couriers and coffee or snack shops in the lobby. Making business operations easier and more efficient for tenants is one of the principal tasks of the office building manager.

According to the 2004 IREM survey, approximately 50 percent of all managers surveyed operate at least some office properties. This number includes managers who work exclusively with office properties and managers who control a mixed portfolio, including residential and commercial properties.

Managing Shopping Centers

Shopping center and retail strip management shares only some similarities with managing an apartment or office building. Although the shopping center manager is responsible for maintenance and leasing, his or her most important job is working with retail tenants to ensure their success. This task is important not only to keep tenants at the center, but also because shopping center leases usually provide that the center's owners receive a percentage of the sales dollars made by merchants. Therefore, successful merchants equal a successful center.

To achieve this goal, the shopping center manager must focus on finding tenants for the center that will appeal to shoppers in the area and complement one another. Before leasing begins on a shopping center, the property manager will develop information on the income, age, and number of people located near the center. By reviewing this information and looking at competing centers in the neighborhood, the manager will be able to decide what kinds of goods and services shoppers want and need. The property manager also will work with the main, or anchor, tenants to determine what the focus of the center will be. A center may focus on convenience tenants, such as a dry cleaner, a hardware store, a shoe repair shop, and a grocery. Or, a center may focus on fashion (with clothing and shoe stores) or entertainment (with movie theaters and restaurants).

Once the focus of the center is decided upon, the manager will try to develop a good tenant mix, choosing stores that do not compete directly with each other but that might attract similar shoppers. Even after the center is leased, the manager must constantly review the tenant mix to ensure that it is the most profitable for the center.

The shopping center manager's support of tenants' sales does not stop with leasing. The manager works with tenants to promote the center and the various stores through advertising and special events sponsored at the center. These events, unlike those at apartment and office properties, are intended to attract shoppers to the center rather than to please the tenants. Centers also maintain extensive websites to attract and inform customers about the center. A strong sense of promotion and an understanding of retail selling are essential to the success of the shopping center manager.

Shopping center management is such a specialized area that, except in less-populated areas, most shopping center managers work exclusively on retail property. In some cases, however, smaller retail strip centers may be managed by those with more mixed portfolios. The 2004 IREM survey estimated that about 26 percent of all its manager members operated some retail properties.

Managing Other Types of Property

In addition to these principal property types often handled by the property manager, almost any type of building can and will require management. Industrial properties are sometimes managed directly by an employee of the company leasing the space. However, the 2004 IREM survey found that 16 percent of its members oversaw the management of industrial properties or industrial parks. Other types of commercial properties that frequently employ managers include warehouse space, medical buildings, and parking garages. The manager may have a slightly different title, but the jobs of maintenance, hiring staff, and controlling operating costs are much the same.

Of course, many property managers manage more than one type of property or change their work emphasis during a career. It's not uncommon to move from one property type to another during the course of a property management career. While each property type requires certain specialized skills, each has many similarities—an attention to detail, the ability to deal with others, and the presence of mind to handle the unexpected.

4

Entering the Property Management Field

Although the field of property management has few formal entry requirements, it is important to get the education and skills you need to succeed in this fast-growing profession.

Licensure

All states and some Canadian provinces require that you have a real estate license if you lease property as a part of your overall property management business. Other provinces require licensure only when selling real estate. Some states require that managers of condominiums also hold real estate licenses. In some cases, this requirement does not extend to residential managers who live on the property. However, it is best to check the requirements of each state. In addition, a real estate license is necessary in all states for property managers or on-site managers who also sell real estate.

Licensing fees range from lows of $30 in North Carolina to highs of $450 for an active broker's license in Connecticut, according to a study by the Association of Real Estate License Law Officials (ARELLO), which serves both United States and Canadian licensing bodies.

All states require prospective licensees to have a high school diploma or equivalent. Today, a high school education is probably the minimum to enter the field of property management.

In addition, the majority of states require that applicants pass a real estate course before taking the licensing examination. These courses vary in length from state to state, ranging from as few as thirty hours up to more than one hundred hours of classroom work. Licensure courses include some study specific to property management, but the principal focus of the class is usually on selling real estate. Licensure classes are offered at many community colleges and universities and at private schools specializing in real estate training. In some cases, real estate companies sponsor courses.

Whether or not prospective licensees are required to take a real estate course, all states require that they pass a written examination for licensure. These one-day tests usually consist of multiple-choice questions in two areas—general real estate and state laws affecting real estate.

The examination covers real estate topics such as:

• **Real estate contracts.** This covers the meaning of various clauses in a contract, the legal obligations of the real estate agent, and the rights of each part to a contract.

• **Leasing.** This covers the meaning of the various lease clauses, state and federal laws protecting the rights of tenants, and leasing techniques.

- **Real estate ownership laws.** This covers the elements of a deed, different ownership rights to land, and fair housing laws.
- **Real estate finance.** This covers the elements of a mortgage and the types of mortgages available.

The test is mostly focused on real estate sales. However, many of the provisions, such as fair housing laws and contracts, also apply to property management.

Examinations are given at regular intervals in different locations in the state. Each state sets its own passing score, usually between seventy and seventy-five out of one hundred. Most states allow an applicant to take the test more than once, if necessary.

Other requirements for licensure also vary by state. Generally, a person must have lived in the state for six months to take the exam and must be eighteen years old.

Because of the efforts of ARELLO, many states will permit a person holding a real estate license in one state to work in another state without having to meet all that state's requirements. However, this is not always true, so it is best to check the individual state's laws.

In general, the trend among state and provincial licensing agencies is to require more education before granting a license. The number of classroom hours are being increased in many jurisdictions, although a few still only require applicants to pass a written exam to obtain a real estate license. Many states also have some requirement that licensees continue to complete courses of study to keep their licenses. Here again, however, most continuing education courses are focused on real estate sales. It is often difficult for the property manager to find courses for continuing education that apply to the management field.

Education

We have already mentioned that a high school diploma is the minimum requirement for entry into this field. Here is a more in-depth discussion of the education needs for success in a property management career.

High School

A 2004 survey by the Institute of Real Estate Management found that approximately 3 percent of respondents had only a high school education. Although it may be possible to obtain a resident manager position with nothing beyond a high school education, the higher-level jobs are more difficult to attain without at least some college study.

Even in high school it is possible to begin developing the skills for success in property management. Property management is a combination of strong math and financial skills and good communications skills with people.

To develop strong financial skills, at least three years of math and perhaps accounting or bookkeeping are extremely useful. Because much of the financial analysis of property management is now done on personal computers, a knowledge of basic programs for computers is also important.

Good communication abilities are equally important to the successful property manager. Good writing skills should be developed, because managers often submit written proposals to potential clients. At least three years of English and perhaps a writing course or work on the school paper could help to develop these skills.

Oral skills are needed to maintain good relationships with tenants, to communicate effectively with owners, and in leasing. In addition to English, speech or drama classes might be a good way to learn to speak more eloquently.

Psychology, economics, and business courses also are useful. In this increasing multicultural country, language skills, especially the ability to speak Spanish, will be valuable in working with both tenants and staff.

High school is also a good place to begin another important element of property management—public contact. Becoming active in school or community groups that interest you is an excellent way to develop future sources of potential tenants and clients.

College

Although property management does not require a college degree, most property managers today have at least some college education. The 2004 IREM survey found that approximately 27 percent of those surveyed had some college work, another 50 percent were college graduates, and another 19 percent held advanced degrees. The college graduate is rapidly becoming the norm in property management.

This trend has been sped up because of the rapid increase in the number of large companies in the property management field. While almost half of property management firms employ fewer than ten people, the number of those that employ more than fifty is growing rapidly.

In addition, more and more large properties now belong to real estate investment trusts, financial institutions, pension funds, and other so-called institutional investors. These large owners may hire a smaller management company to manage a local property, but they are much more likely to require a college degree than is a small property owner.

At present there are approximately sixty-one U.S. colleges that offer a major in real estate leading to a bachelor's degree, according to *Peterson's Four Year Colleges*. In addition, several Canadian colleges and universities offer real estate education at the college level (see Appendix A). Although only a few colleges (notably Ball State University and Virginia Tech) currently have specific property management majors, many more are adding courses in the field, according to a spokesperson from the Institute of Real Estate Management.

Distance-learning options online are another source of real estate education. The Professional Career Development Institute is one source of distance-learning courses on property management. Visit universities.com/distance_learning for more sources. Many community colleges and private real estate schools also offer associate degrees or course work in real estate.

Real estate majors generally focus on real estate finance, appraisal, or development. However, the courses in economics, investment, and market research included in these majors also will be valuable to the property manager.

Even without a major in real estate, college work may be focused on the needs of property management. A major in business administration, economics, accounting, or a related field would be excellent preparation for the financial aspects of property management.

To prepare for the communications aspects of the property management business, college students may study communications, speech, English, psychology, and advertising/public relations.

Whatever the area of study, college course work should help the individual learn to work independently, locate and synthesize information, and communicate ideas to others. All of these skills will help ensure success in property management.

Universities that offer advanced degrees in real estate often maintain real estate centers that conduct research on real estate activity in their state. If there is such a center in your area, it is probably an excellent source of information on market conditions and laws affecting real estate.

Professional Organizations

Because of the relative lack of academic courses on property management, many beginning property managers learn about the field from courses taught by the country's many property management associations. These educational offerings may vary from one-day seminars up to courses of forty or fifty hours. Courses and seminars also provide ongoing education for those already in the field. A comprehensive list of real estate management associations appears in Appendix B.

Building Owners and Managers Association

The Building Owners and Managers Association (BOMA) is an association for office building managers, owners, and investors. The association has chapters in the United States and Canada and offers three professional designations—the real property administrator, the facilities management administrator, and the systems maintenance administrator. The courses leading to these designations include such important areas as laws for property management, the operation and design of building systems, accounting and financial concepts, energy management, refrigeration and heating repair, and supervision. In addition, BOMA publishes *Skylines*, a monthly newsletter on industry techniques and trends, and holds annual meetings and seminars on timely topics.

Canadian Real Estate Association

The Canadian Real Estate Association (CREA) represents more than eighty-eight thousand real estate brokers/agents and salespeople as well as those working in related real estate fields, such as property management and appraisal. It also operates a residential multiple-listing service of homes for sale as well as a commercial listing site.

Community Associations Institute

The Community Associations Institute (CAI) offers a designation for persons who complete its courses in condominium management and meet certain other qualifying requirements. CAI also publishes newsletters focusing on legal issues in community management.

CoreNet Global

CoreNet Global was formed by merging the International Development Research Council and the National Association of Corporate Real Estate Executives. The organization focuses on the global use of real estate assets by corporations. Its membership consists of corporate real estate executives, service providers to those corporations, and economic developers from various governmental agencies.

It conducts regular meetings and development seminars both live and on the Web. CoreNet Global offers a Master of Corporate Real Estate (MCR) designation for senior managers and a Senior Leader in Corporate Real Estate (SLCR) certificate. In 2004 it published a series of research studies entitled "Corporate Real Estate 2010" that explores the future of the industry.

International Council of Shopping Centers

As its name implies, the International Council of Shopping Centers (ICSC) specializes in courses relating to shopping center management. Its members are owners, developers, retailers, suppliers, and managers of shopping centers.

Through its University of Shopping Centers and other educational offerings, ICSC offers seminars on leasing and operating centers. Publications and a monthly magazine provide vital knowledge.

ICSC offers several professional designations, including certified shopping center manager and certified marketing director.

International Facilities Management Association

Members of the International Facilities Management Association (IFMA) work primarily for corporations or large nonprofit institutions, such as hospitals or universities. IFMA holds regular conferences and publishes research reports.

The IFMA awards the Certified Facility Manager (CFM) designation. To qualify, members must combine education and experience and pass an exam of competency in finance, communications, and operations. Designation holders must also complete continuing education requirements every three years. In 2006 there were approximately 18,500 IFMA members.

Institute of Real Estate Management

The Institute of Real Estate Management (IREM) is a professional association for property managers in the United States and Canada. Unlike most other property management trade associations, IREM members may manage any or all types of property. Of course, some of its members specialize in one major property type. Also, unlike the other associations discussed above, members of IREM must complete several educational courses and other requirements before being admitted to membership. All members hold the certified property manager designation.

IREM's courses include management business operations; leasing and operating apartments, offices, or shopping centers; and financial analysis and decision making. A separate course for on-site apartment managers may lead to the accredited residential manager recognition award. The association also offers special seminars on specific management topics.

IREM publishes numerous books on property management, including *The Principles of Real Estate Management*, which is still considered to be the basic book in the field. The *Journal of Property Management* is published six times a year. Two annual conventions with education sessions round out IREM's educational offerings.

National Apartment Association

The National Apartment Association (NAA) offers courses and seminars through its national organization and through many state and local chapters. The organization offers courses for the apartment manager, the federally assisted housing manager, the apartment property supervisor, the leasing agent, and the maintenance worker. Each of these areas can lead to a special designation certificate granted by the NAA. The association also maintains a lending library of books and articles relating to the apartment industry and publishes a monthly magazine, *Units*.

National Property Management Association, Inc.

Established in 1970, this group's members are primarily employees of federal agencies or their contractor counterparts. However, they also manage property for universities, health care institutions, and manufacturing companies. The group offers educational courses nationwide and recognizes best practices in the property management field.

Real Estate Institute of Canada

The Real Estate Institute of Canada (REIC) is a nonprofit organization with members that perform a variety of real estate specialties, including property management. REIC's property management section is affiliated with the Institute of Real Estate Management and offers the certified property manager (CPM) designation with most of the same criteria used in the United States. Courses developed by IREM are taught by Canadian instructors, who have adapted materials to meet Canadian needs. REIC also publishes a magazine on property management issues.

The other associations and private educational companies offering property management–related courses are too numerous to describe in detail here. However, most associations listed in Appendix B present at least occasional educational offerings in their specific areas.

Experience

Despite the many associations offering courses and designations, much of what a property manager knows is learned on the job.

Therefore, gaining some exposure to the management field will be of great benefit in pursuing a property management career.

Summer or part-time employment as a maintenance worker at an apartment complex or as a clerical worker in a management office are two ways to learn more about management. In some cases, owners of small buildings may look for a college student or part-time worker to manage a small building in exchange for rent. Often these jobs do not require licensure and are an excellent opportunity to perform many of the functions of property management on a simpler scale.

Quite a few property managers come to the field from residential brokerage. They gain some management experience by supervising management of single-family homes and smaller buildings during the period they are for sale. Some workers find that they prefer the more consistent income of property management to the uncertainty of selling.

Other areas that offer experience related to property management include retail sales, banking, law, and construction.

Another key way to prepare for a career in property management is to gain a good knowledge of the community—how people shop, where they live, the location of businesses and stores. Establishing good business and personal contacts in the community through clubs, sports, or volunteer work is also a good foundation for a job in property management.

As with any field, education does not ensure success. However, a well-rounded education with emphasis on both financial and communications skills is a terrific first step in entering the field of property management.

5

Factors Affecting Real Estate

REGARDLESS OF THE type of property you manage or how high you rise in the field, the job outlook in property management depends on the overall strength of the local, national, and international real estate and financial markets. By understanding the influences that affect real estate building, sales, and occupancy, the prospective property manager can understand how and when opportunities arise.

The economic health of real estate is influenced by the strength of the overall economy. When employment is high, people have more money to spend at shopping centers and to pay as rent on apartments. When businesses are growing, they need more office, warehouse, and industrial space. The strength of real estate markets depends on the economic strength of the country.

And because real estate is permanent and cannot be moved like other types of goods, the economic conditions of the area in which it is located also have a tremendous effect on its value. For example, office vacancies in Dallas might increase because of overbuilding. Yet, the empty offices in Dallas cannot be moved to Boston, where the demand might be high. Real estate still remains a local market in many ways.

The economic and social influences that affect real estate are changing, however. Understanding these influences may help to understand the present and the future of property management.

Globalization of the Real Estate Industry

As just mentioned, real estate and real estate management have historically been local industries. Unlike many other goods, real estate could not be moved from one place to another.

Because of its local nature, the real estate industry also was primarily organized along local lines. Most companies specialized in one or two cities and became experts in those areas. Knowledge about local markets was acquired through fairly random means and was closely guarded by each company as a way to offer the best service to clients.

However, beginning in the 1980s and continuing through today, this local model has changed somewhat. Although real estate is still not portable, thanks to the Internet and the data capacity of modern computers, vast amounts of information are available almost anywhere on the globe. This availability decreases the market advantage of local firms. Nonetheless, most real estate is still owned by smaller, local owners.

Unlike some industries, very little real estate activity has been outsourced overseas. Some architectural companies use offshore sources to update blueprints, but the lack of standardization in commercial real estate leases and sales contracts makes it difficult for workers not familiar with local real estate customs and language to perform duties such as summarizing leases, called *lease abstracting*, and other routine functions. However, quite a number of real estate trade groups and vendors are working toward creating standardized real estate terms used in leases and sales contracts. The main reason for this push toward standardization is to make totally electronic transactions possible. If groups such as the Open Standards Consortium for Real Estate and the Mortgage Industry Standards Maintenance Organization coalitions are successful in creating widely accepted definitions, it will also make it much easier to outsource clerical and analytical functions overseas.

Growth of Publicly Owned Real Estate

The decade of the 1990s was one of profound and lasting change for real estate. The field has been transformed from a primarily local, private industry to one that is increasingly public and global. One of the most significant factors causing this change has been the rise in real estate investment trusts (REITs) and the decision by many real estate companies to become public companies and sell stock on the stock exchanges. While the number of REITs fell for a while from its highs in the mid-1990s, there were 197 REITs at the end of 2005, according to the National Association of Real Estate Investment Trusts. More important, the value of the REIT market has grown tremendously in the last decade, with equity REITs (those that own property as opposed to mortgages) reaching a value of more than $330 billion in 2005.

REITs today are held by both large portfolio managers and small investors and play a significant ongoing role in the real estate industry. REIT mutual funds make it possible for smaller investors to own investment real estate. At the other end of the investment spectrum, pension funds are also using REIT ownership as a complement to owning individual properties.

While in recent years there has been a minor trend toward some REIT shareholders taking companies private, REITs are too well established to be ignored.

Continuing Flow of Capital

Commercial real estate income is derived from two principal sources: operating income in the form of rents and increases in the value of the buildings, called *appreciation*. While property managers focus most of their activities on rents and other regular income generated by properties, both factors are important to investors. In recent years, rents have not been growing for many property types. However, strong investor interest among both private and institutional owners as well as foreign investors have helped boost real estate prices to very high levels. This flow of capital to commercial real estate is expected to keep prices strong for the next several years. In addition, for most commercial properties, many experts believe rents will go up and vacancies will drop.

Another major contributor to the flow of capital into commercial real estate is the growth of the commercial mortgage-backed securities (CMBS) market. CMBSs are public securities backed by the payments on a group of mortgages issued on apartments, office buildings, or other commercial, income-producing properties. A similar practice has been in place for residential mortgages for several decades. However, because almost every commercial loan has unique features, while residential loans are fairly uniform, the commercial market took much longer to evolve. Today, the CMBS market provides a way for banks and other lenders to "sell" their loans and gain new funds to make additional loans. In 2005 the CMBS market accounted for more than $700 billion in funds flowing to commercial real estate, according to the Commercial Mortgage Backed Securities Association. In large part, it is this increased availability of capital that has helped strengthen commercial real estate prices.

Consolidation of Real Estate

As has been the case with U.S. industries ranging from steel to banking, the real estate services industry has undergone significant consolidation in recent decades, although large firms still control a relatively small share of the overall commercial real estate market. What was essentially a local industry has seen mergers that created regional, national, and even international companies that offer a full range of real estate services.

Several factors have contributed to this trend:

• **More institutional ownership.** Because a significant portion of investment-grade real estate is now owned by larger owners such as pension funds, banks, real estate investment trusts, and private real estate companies that function on a national level, there is an increased demand for companies that can meet needs nationwide. A company that can provide service in ten cities is more efficient to employ than ten companies doing business in one city each.

• **One-stop shopping.** These same large owners also want to improve efficiency by contracting with firms that can provide a wide range of real estate services, such as purchasing, construction, management, and sales. A large service firm is in a better position to provide all of these services within one organization.

- **Technology.** Like many industries, success in real estate requires regular, expensive computer upgrades. A larger company is in a better position to absorb the cost of technology upgrades and to spread that cost across more and more customers.
- **Globalization.** As real estate owners and investors increasingly look for opportunities worldwide and foreign investors again become investors in U.S. real estate (thanks to a falling dollar), a firm that can provide international service is at a distinct competitive advantage. Although many firms have made forays into international markets, only a few have succeeded. The significant differences in real estate laws and customs, as well as severe overbuilding and economic fluctuations in some markets, have made success in the foreign arena hard to achieve. However, the potential rewards are such that U.S. firms are likely to continue overseas activities, making foreign language skills—especially Spanish and Chinese—very appealing to employers.

Larger firms generally offer a range of services, including property management, construction, leasing, and sales. Although the work done by these firms is similar in many ways to that done by local firms, there are some differences. Because they operate nationally, larger firms generally have more career-advancement options than smaller firms can offer. Opportunities may also exist to move to a different part of the country, or even overseas. As a general rule, large companies have more funds for training and benefits than do smaller ones, so employees may have more support in building their careers.

At the same time, large national firms have some negatives. A national scope of business may require more travel than a small local firm, and transfers to different parts of the country may place burdens on family members. Working national also makes it harder to establish ties in a particular community and develop the contacts and in-depth market knowledge that can make a manager's job easier.

Changing Demographics

The aging of the 78.2 million baby boomers in the United States, as well as an aging population in Canada, will have a tremendous economic effect on all aspects of real estate in the years ahead. In the housing sector, some boomers are moving to more urban locations and renting apartments or buying condominiums. The strong move back to downtowns is also creating demand for retail properties in central city locations. Other buyers, mostly nearing retirement, are purchasing second homes in resort locations. Many of these properties will require management as well as leasing agents to rent out second homes to vacationers. Most experts also expect a growing demand for independent-living and assisted-living facilities for the elderly. Although this type of management often requires health care as well as real estate skills, the area promises to grow significantly in the next decades.

Apartments should also perform well in the next decade, as the children of baby boomers enter their twenties and begin to live independently. The "echo boomers," or Generation Y, number about seventy-one million. Multifamily properties also should be in demand for families that cannot afford to pay the ever-rising price of a single-family home. Thus higher interest rates will make it more attractive for some people to rent rather than buy a home.

Immigrants, who play an important role in population expansion in both the United States and Canada, are also more inclined to begin as renters. In Canada, 60 percent of population growth between 2001 and 2006 was the result of foreign immigration. In the United States, approximately 25 percent of the population growth between the middle of 2000 and the middle of 2006 was the result of foreign immigration, according to the U.S. Census Bureau.

Another trend that may increase the need for property managers in the next decade is the growth of multipurpose communities that incorporate residential, retail, and sometimes office properties in one large development. These communities, which are sometimes called *new urban* communities, seek to mirror small-town life by providing walkable living areas, mass transit, and shared community parks and green space. Although much of the housing in new urban communities is owner occupied, such properties often require the services of one or more managers to oversee community activities and to lease retail and office space.

Many experts also believe that changes in demographics and technology will alter the demand for office space in the years ahead. As technology has made it easier to communicate effectively from many locations, more and more corporations are letting some employees work from remote sites. A shortage of workers as baby boomers retire may also make it easier for workers to negotiate off-site work alternatives. Some companies no longer assign specific desks to each worker but let them choose any open space. There is also a trend among companies to reduce the amount of office space assigned to each worker. Electronic storage also reduces the amount of space needed for files. Nevertheless, most companies will still need office space for meetings and to create a sense of corporate culture, so office space demand should not be severely affected.

Likewise, while some experts predicted that Internet selling would be the end of retail, shopping center owners have seen demand grow and rents rise in recent years. Consumers not only like to buy in person, but they are drawn to the movies, restaurants, and other entertainment options that are becoming a bigger part of retail properties.

Strong Economy, Strong Real Estate Market

Like every business, real estate and property management are affected by economic and population trends, social concerns, and natural and manmade factors. Yet despite fluctuating economic conditions, the role of the property manager remains a secure part of the real estate industry. A good property manager will still have opportunities for growth and advancement no matter what the economic climate.

6

On-Site Manager

For those interested in working their way up the property management ladder, a good point of entry is that of residential on-site manager or assistant on-site manager. While not all on-site apartment managers actually live on the site, a significant number still live at the building they manage.

According to a 2004 survey of its accredited residential managers (ARMs) conducted by the Institute of Real Estate Management, approximately 56 percent of residential managers work at privately financed apartments. Approximately 22 percent work at federally assisted housing properties. Residential managers may also manage condominiums, housing for the elderly, or any other type of residential property.

Office buildings, shopping centers, and other types of property may have on-site managers, provided the property is large enough to justify the cost. Regardless of the property type, the responsibilities of the on-site manager are similar.

The on-site manager oversees many of the daily operations involved in the management and leasing of a property. While few on-site managers are solely responsible for developing budgets, they do receive and record rent checks and issue late-rent notices and other billings.

The on-site manager also handles petty cash and signs for deliveries of goods and services ordered for the building. In some cases, the on-site manager buys routinely required items and services such as lawn care and cleaning products, trash removal, and plumbing and minor maintenance. In the case of larger buildings, especially offices and shopping centers, the on-site manager hires and supervises the work of maintenance workers and clerical personnel.

The on-site manager's job requires that he or she be at the site most of the time, ready to handle tenant complaints and to visit tenants in an ongoing program of building good tenant relations.

Job Description

According to the 2004 IREM survey, approximately 60 percent of accredited residential property managers work for property management companies. Approximately 10 percent each work for private property owners and full-service real estate companies. Another 5 percent work for investment or trust companies.

The IREM survey of its ARM members also found that the typical member manages approximately 320 units, although 29 percent manage more than 600 units. Most also supervise staff, with a median of nine employees supervised.

Because the on-site manager is the person responsible for the daily operation of the property, he or she is often on call twenty-four hours a day. Larger properties rotate evening and weekend on-call responsibilities. When an emergency or problem arises, the on-site manager must handle the incident quickly and effectively. A cool head and good communication skills are essential.

The on-site manager serves as the direct link between tenants and management; indeed, most tenants rarely come in contact with any other part of the management company. A concern for people, a dedication to service, and an outgoing personality help the on-site manager create a positive image of the property and the management company for the tenant. Good tenant relations is the backbone of the on-site manager's job and a vital part of the overall success of the property's management.

Education

The on-site manager is less likely than the property or portfolio manager to have a college degree. According to the 2004 IREM survey, about 51 percent of the residential managers surveyed had some college work, while 27 percent held a college degree and 8 percent a graduate degree. Approximately 14 percent held a high school diploma. However, there was a correlation between the amount of education an on-site manager had and the level of earnings he or she received.

As noted earlier, on-site managers may not need to hold a real estate license. However, licensure is still a good step for future advancement.

Earnings

According to the 2004 IREM survey, total earnings for the residential managers surveyed averaged $53,574 annually. This figure included a salary of $47,369 as well as bonuses, commissions, and sometimes free apartment rent. Earnings are generally higher in the Northeast and Pacific areas, but the variation is small.

Another survey by CEL & Associates, a full-service consulting firm for the real estate industry, revealed that residential site managers at properties with more than three hundred units earned $52,200. Those managing fewer than three hundred units had a median income of $40,600. In 2005, Canadian property administrators had average salaries of $18.10 (Canadian dollars) per hour in the Toronto area, according to the www.labourmarketinforma tion.ca website, which is maintained by Service Canada. The site also includes salary breakdowns for other provinces.

Profile of an Apartment Manager

Shirley Ellis's career as an apartment manager began when she took over temporary responsibility of two apartment buildings owned by her husband's ailing father. Ellis became "sort of manager, den mother, and friend" to the college students who rented rooms on the property.

Ellis was only twenty-two, not much older than the students, but to help out her family, she had to keep everything running smoothly. Then she found out she liked doing it.

Once her father-in-law's health returned, Ellis went back to a more conventional job. However, fate seemed determined that she become a residential manager.

Several years later, Ellis became close friends with the manager of a small apartment property where she was living. When the manager left, she suggested that Ellis be given the job. Fifteen years later, Ellis is still in the property management field.

Ellis likes the change and challenge of management. "You can't be a successful on-site manager unless you enjoy being interrupted," she jokes.

Today, Ellis manages the two-hundred-unit Sturbridge Apartments, which is located in an affluent area of Little Rock, Arkansas. She supervises five full-time staff members, including a leasing agent, an assistant manager, a maintenance person, and a painter. When she first began supervising people, she had a hard time delegating jobs.

Although Ellis believes that on-the-job training is still the way most on-site managers learn, she found that formal training, such as the on-site manager course offered by the Institute of Real Estate Management that she took some years after entering the field, can help managers greatly expand their skills. And Ellis says no matter how long a manager is in the field, there's always something new to learn.

Ellis also believes that the quality of the company a property manager works for has a big impact on management success. She has found that a strong management company offers a valuable source of information, as well as a comrade with which to share problems.

The increased professionalism of the on-site manager's job is something that excites Ellis. At her first job, she says, the office was right next to her apartment. "If I had to show an apartment, I would just run next door in my blue jeans and with rollers in my hair." Today, however, the image projected is more professional. Property managers have to be more sophisticated, because tenants are much more aware of their rights, and managers have to be current. Young people considering a career in property management should realize how much they need to know to succeed, she concludes.

Outlook

Although the 2004 IREM survey reveals that many resident managers plan to move up the property management ladder, others like the job of on-site manager. The average accredited residential manager (ARM) has thirteen years of real estate experience. More than 81 percent of those surveyed by IREM have seven or more years of management experience in the on-site management field.

As apartment living remains a viable option for those who cannot afford or do not want home ownership, the demand for well-trained residential managers will continue to grow. Whether the job of on-site manager is a stepping-stone to something else or a lifetime career, it offers great challenges and rewards for the manager.

7

LEASING BROKER

UNTIL RECENTLY, THE on-site or property manager handled the majority of rental property leasing. Indeed, leasing activities in many residential properties and smaller office buildings are still carried out by the property manager.

However, in many apartments, office buildings, and strip shopping centers, leasing has become a specialized activity. In some cases, leasing agents work directly for the property management company. These leasing agents are generally assigned leasing responsibilities for one or more buildings at a time, depending on the size of the units. Often leasing agents, like property managers, specialize in one type of property.

The leasing agent usually concentrates all of his or her time marketing and leasing the property. These properties may be new constructions or older buildings with a high vacancy rate. In either case, the leasing agent's responsibility is to locate sound tenants for the buildings as quickly as possible.

Another category of leasing agent, usually called a *commercial broker*, works as an independent agent for a management company or property owner. A commercial broker may be self-employed or work for a firm or division of a company that specializes in leasing. In some instances, commercial leasing activities are handled by firms that also sell commercial property. As the name implies, commercial brokers are most often active in leasing office buildings and shopping centers.

The commercial broker's only responsibility is to locate tenants for the building. The commercial broker is not responsible for property operations or ongoing tenant relations.

Although the commercial broker usually works as an agent of the property owner, he or she may also be employed by a business tenant looking for space. This specialty is called *tenant brokerage*. In these instances, the broker acts as a consultant, using his or her market knowledge to find spaces appropriate to a client's needs. Large companies and businesses moving to a new area may be most likely to employ a tenant broker familiar with the local market. However, many firms find that the commercial broker's market awareness saves them time and money.

Job Description

The commercial leasing broker uses available market research to determine the best possible tenants for a property. Many firms that specialize in commercial leasing employ full-time research personnel to develop such market data.

The broker or leasing agent then begins to locate tenants who meet this marketing profile. Brokers will determine the amount of space a prospective tenant needs and any special requirements for the space, such as strong floors for heavy equipment. The location and accessibility of a property also influence the type of tenant it may attract.

For example, a smaller, less-opulent office building located near an airport and an expressway might be ideal for a sales company. Salespeople need to travel often and usually see potential customers at the customer's place of business. Therefore, the appearance of the sales company's office is probably less important than it would be to a law firm or other business that sees clients at its office.

Because tenants are concerned about the financial costs of the rented space, leasing agents must be able to compare the costs of maintenance, heating, and other charges in a building with that of the competition. Thus, a good basic understanding of the building's operations and finances is essential.

However, the leasing agent or commercial broker is still primarily a salesperson. Skills in psychology, marketing, and communications are vital for successful selling. A determined yet friendly personality also helps put prospects at ease. Finally, any salesperson must be able to handle rejection and keep trying.

In many cases, the leasing agent also participates in the actual lease negotiations, although seldom does the agent have the power to sign the lease for larger commercial properties. Still, he or she needs a basic knowledge of lease provisions and their implications. Strong negotiating skills are important. Today properties for lease are often posted on the Web, and all or part of a lease negotiation may be handled via e-mail.

Education

Specific formal education, with the exception of a real estate license, is not usually necessary to work as a leasing agent or commercial broker. However, classes in marketing, advertising, market research, finance, and public speaking offer good preparation. Time spent learning about the local real estate market is equally valuable.

Quite often leasing agents gain experience in real estate sales before moving into leasing. Work in market research also may be a useful starting place to enter the field. At the same time, as already mentioned, knowledge of lease clauses and their implications, building operations, and financial analysis must be a part of the commercial broker's overall training.

There are few formal courses on leasing with the exception of a few taught by some of the associations mentioned in Chapter 4. However, courses on property management and general selling skills will probably be helpful. Some people believe the ability to sell is inborn. However, specific selling techniques and market knowledge to back up selling will greatly improve a leasing agent's chances of success.

Earnings

Earnings for leasing brokers vary widely depending on the size of the properties leased and on whether the agent is an employee of a property management firm or is an independent agent.

Leasing agents working for a property management firm often receive a salary and a commission or bonus based on the amount of property leased. The U.S. Bureau of Labor Statistics found that the median annual salary for lessors of real estate in 2004 was $34,300. A 2006 survey by CEL & Associates indicated that leasing agents at office and industrial properties earned median annual earnings of $58,200. Leasing representatives at residential properties earned a median of $25,500. Those at retail properties earned a median of $78,400.

According to a 2006 survey by the Building Owners and Managers Association, Calgary, approximately half of the leasing agents for office buildings earned between $90,000 and $100,000 (Canadian dollars) before commissions, while the remaining half earned less than $70,000 before commissions. (Keep in mind that the Calgary market was very strong during the period of the survey, and earnings in other areas may be somewhat less.)

Statistics Canada estimated that salaries for commercial leasing brokers and rental agents rose by about 18 percent between 2001 and 2004. However, income for residential leasing agents fell by 50 percent during the same period. Commissions earned for leasing at residential properties often take the form of a specific amount paid for each lease that is signed. Some companies also offer this bonus to property management personnel who lease as part of their regular activities.

Commercial brokers for office and shopping center properties are more likely to receive a percentage of the lease amount as earnings. These percentages vary widely, depending on the difficulty of leasing in a specific market. However, even a 5 percent commission on a lease for $100,000 is a significant amount. Of course, an income based on commissions is less steady and dependable than a monthly salary. And because larger commercial leases may take several months to negotiate, periods between commissions may be long.

Generally, leasing agents employed by a property company or a commercial broker working in the leasing division of a full-service real estate company receive such standard benefits as group hospitalization, paid vacation, and life insurance. Commercial brokers may also receive such benefits as a company car or a regular expense account to assist them in their work.

Profile of a Leasing Broker/Property Manager

Deborah Chapman's father was a contractor, so she had an early knowledge of real estate, but it wasn't until after she entered college and took a real estate course that Chapman decided that commercial real estate was for her—even though she recognized that it was a more difficult way to break into the business than managing residential properties.

Chapman worked for an advertising agency briefly after college, and after sending out many letters of inquiry, she was offered a job as an assistant property manager and leasing agent at a small office building.

Left on her own, Chapman began learning about property management through trial and error. She leased property all day and then took the leases home at night to study them. She also took several property management courses. The hard work paid off, and the building was soon well occupied.

Unlike many leasing brokers, Chapman handles both the property management and leasing for the four buildings she now supervises. She believes that each area of management is interesting and that leasing and management complement each other.

She likes property management because it always pays a base salary. In leasing, the agent is much more dependent on commissions. She also finds that leasing is more stressful. "In property management, you make clear progress and can look back on achievement," she says.

Chapman also thinks that being responsible for management affects her leasing efforts. Unlike most leasing brokers, who are through with a transaction when the lease is signed, she has to live with the tenant afterward. This makes her more concerned about finding the right tenant for the space, she says.

Chapman's position with a smaller company also enables her to try new things. She feels that she is less locked into a hierarchy and can experiment more than if she were employed at a larger, more structured company.

Outlook

Because tenants constantly relocate and the demand for space continues to increase and decrease with the economy, there will always be a need for leasing brokers. The U.S. Bureau of Labor Statistics estimates the demand for real estate leasing agents will increase by 22 percent between 2004 and 2014, growing to approximately thirty-six thousand positions.

Leasing offers a unique niche in the field of property management. As management, especially at higher levels, focuses more and more on finance and analysis, leasing offers the opportunity of personal contact and flexibility.

8

PROPERTY MANAGER

THROUGHOUT THIS BOOK we use the term *property manager* to describe an individual who performs any of the leasing or operations functions associated with a real estate property. In this chapter, *property manager* will be used in a more specific way.

A property manager, sometimes called a *property supervisor*, is responsible for the ongoing operation of several different properties or, in a few cases, of one very large property. He or she visits the properties and evaluates the performance of the on-site manager. He or she helps to establish management policies and plans for the property and works to ensure that the property is running smoothly. The property manager has at least some participation in planning the yearly budgets for properties and usually has day-to-day responsibilities for seeing that these budgets are met. Approximately 29 percent of the members surveyed in the 2004 IREM study worked as property supervisors.

The *executive-level property manager* is also discussed in this chapter. The executive-level property manager supervises the work of the property supervisors in his or her employ. This manager is often the head of a property management department or a president or vice president of a fee management firm. Approximately 29 percent of managers in the 2004 IREM survey were classified as either a regional/district manager or an officer/director, probably indicating their status as executive-level managers.

Job Description

The executive manager reviews the work of each property supervisor and steps in if significant problems occur. The executive manager also generally serves as the principal contact with the property's owner or with the senior management of the real estate company. Working with the owner, the executive manager sets financial goals for the property, identifies and analyzes major maintenance and renovation projects, and approves all management policies and controls for the property. He or she may also analyze property revenue options to find ways to enhance the property's income and value. Finally, the executive-level property manager is often responsible for securing new business for the firm or department.

Of course, the distinction between these two levels is seldom clear-cut. In a smaller firm, an executive-level manager is more likely to also handle some property supervision. At a large company, the executive manager probably has little direct contact with the tenants or on-site management staffs, unless a major problem arises.

The skills and knowledge needed by the property manager and the executive property manager are much the same: a thorough knowledge of property operations, leasing, budgeting and financial analysis, supervision, and tenant relations.

Property Supervisor

The job of property supervisor probably involves more direct contact with tenants than does the executive property manager position. The property supervisor visits each property frequently and is often present during special events. Thus, he or she is the representative of the building's owner to the tenants.

The property supervisor must also be adept at motivating and evaluating the performance of a wide variety of people, from the on-site manager to the maintenance staff. The supervisor generally makes the hiring and firing decisions for the property, so the ability to accurately assess performance is key. At the same time, because the property supervisor is not at the property every day, he or she must delegate responsibilities well and be skilled at training on-site managers to handle daily operations effectively.

The property supervisor also serves as the eyes and ears of the management firm in analyzing the appearance and performance of the property in relation to local competition. The supervisor must understand market conditions and communicate them accurately.

Executive Property Manager

The principal focus of the executive property manager's responsibilities is in the area of finance, long-range planning, and client contact. Because the executive manager visits a property so infrequently, he or she gains much of the information about the property by reviewing operating statements, rent rolls, and tenant lease summaries submitted by the property supervisor.

The executive manager is charged with analyzing those data and determining ways that the property's financial performance might be improved. This improvement might take the form of tighter controls on spending, more effective leasing efforts, a renovation to make the property more competitive, or a change in the property's staff. Therefore, the executive property manager must have a good working knowledge of all aspects of property management. Indeed, most executive property managers have worked their way up from a position as a supervisor or even an on-site manager. He or she must also be a strong supervisor able to motivate others.

The executive property manager uses the financial and lease data he or she receives to develop short- and long-range plans for the property. These long-range plans involve both projections of how the area's real estate market will perform in the future and a wide-ranging analysis of the impact of many possible courses of action on the profitability of the property. The profitable operations and/or sale of the property is always the manager's long-range goal.

Finally, the executive property manager acts as the principal contact with current owners and as the main developer of new management business. Involvement in community activities and professional real estate organizations is particularly important at this level. In addition, the executive manager must combine selling skills with the ability to accurately interpret an owner's goals.

Education

Moving up to the job of property supervisor or executive property manager is possible but difficult without formal real estate education. Although a college degree in a real estate subject may not be necessary for a property supervisor, it is certainly desirable, especially for larger national firms. The property supervisor generally will have completed some real estate courses offered by professional associations or graduate schools. In addition, the supervisor will have had several years of work experience in the real estate management area.

In some cases, qualified on-site managers are promoted to property supervisors. However, such promotions are more difficult to achieve without formal training in today's sophisticated property management field. Frequently, want ads for property supervisors will require that applicants hold a professional designation from one of the real estate associations listed in Appendix B.

Formal real estate education and college-level business is even more important for individuals who want to become executive property managers. Formerly, some supervisors without a college degree may have achieved this level because of their exceptional abilities. However, for those entering the field today, a college degree is essential. The exception to this rule may be the property manager who starts his or her own company and thus becomes the executive. For the individual interested in advancing to an executive level at a larger firm, a real estate education both before and after college is vital.

Executive property managers must have sophisticated financial skills to interpret property information. Computer knowledge is critical in performing long-range projections with spreadsheet, lease, and financial analysis software programs. Marketing and public relations knowledge assists executive managers in promoting the image of the company to future clients, as well as keeping current clients happy.

In a 2004 survey of its membership, which consists of both property supervisors and executive property managers, the Institute of Real Estate Management found that just 3 percent of its members had only a high school degree. Slightly less than 70 percent had completed an undergraduate or advanced college degree.

Earnings

Earnings levels for property managers vary widely depending on the size of the properties managed and the level of executive authority. The U.S. Bureau of Labor Statistics found that property, real estate, and community association managers earned a median of $39,980 in 2004. Those managers working for local governments earned the highest median salary, $51,980.

A 2006 survey by CEL & Associates found that property managers at office/industrial properties of fewer than five hundred thousand square feet had a median income of $63,700. Managers at office/industrial properties larger than one million square feet had median annual earnings of $95,200. District managers for multifamily properties earned a median of $74,900, while those managing retail varied between $67,800 and $93,200, depending upon the size of the property.

A 2006 survey by the Building Owners and Managers Association, Calgary, found that property managers had salaries of between $60,000 and $70,000 (Canadian dollars). In the same survey, senior property managers had salaries between $80,000 and $90,000. Property administrators were also surveyed; they earned between $40,000 and $49,900.

The averages in the 2004 IREM survey, which includes both U.S. and Canadian members, show median earnings of $95,000. In addition to a base salary of $81,256, this figure included commissions on leasing and sales of $25,834. However, only 30 percent of those responding had significant income from commissions.

IREM also surveyed the salaries of individuals who were candidates for its property manager designation. This group, which overall had less experience than IREM members, had median annual earnings of $72,994.

In the IREM survey, salaries were highest among those property managers who worked for investment or trust companies ($107,459 per year) and development/construction companies ($95,270 per year). Those who worked for not-for-profit agencies received the lowest earnings ($68,250 per year). Those working for property management companies had median annual earnings of $89,112; those at full-service real estate companies earned $91,656.

Managers working in conventional apartments had the highest earnings with a median of $97,711, followed by those working on office properties, who earned $94,413. Lower salaries were earned by those managing community associations ($84,828).

According to the 2004 IREM survey, size of the management portfolio has a much greater impact on salary. Managers overseeing fewer than one thousand conventional apartment units received median annual earnings of $78,215, while those supervising more than three thousand units received median annual earnings of $124,761.

Similarly, property managers overseeing fewer than fifty thousand square feet of commercial space received median annual earnings of $78,344, while those managing more than four million square feet received $128,264. In both cases, the increased portfolio size reflects more executive responsibility and more employees under supervision.

Earnings for those certified property managers (CPMs) who had achieved graduate degrees were also 30 percent higher than for those who held only a high school diploma. This statistic might indicate that they had achieved a higher level of authority or worked for a larger company where salaries are generally higher.

Statistics Canada indicates that salaries for property managers have risen by 58 percent between 2001 and 2005.

Profile of a Property Manager

Julie Muir, CPM, a property manager with Elliot Associates Inc., in Portland, Oregon, always knew she wanted to be in real estate, although she didn't realize it was going to be property management. Muir's stepfather was a real estate appraiser, but no one had ever talked about property management with her.

Muir's first job out of high school was as a receptionist in a property management firm. After three years, she decided to learn more about the industry and moved to a property management company that handled a variety of property types, including office and industrial. When an opening at an enclosed mall became available, Muir jumped at the chance to learn about something new. She found she loved managing retail property. A woman at her company soon became her mentor, teacher, and friend. When the property was sold, Muir spent ten productive years in residential management but then decided to return to retail and joined a company that specialized in it. Muir says she likes retail, because it gives her the ability to work with both local and national tenants. She oversees not only the physical assets but also the leasing, marketing, and financial analysis for twenty-seven properties in the western United States—from Alaska to North Dakota.

Muir believes that success in property management takes a lot of common sense, good organizational skills, and the ability to deal with people in difficult situations. "You're often the buffer between a disgruntled tenant and the owner. You have to be the mediator and the problem solver," she says.

The fun part, says Muir, is the property manager's opportunity to take an underperforming property and turn it into a winner. If a property has problems, managers can apply their knowledge to increase its value and profitability and can immediately see results.

Profile of a Vice President of Property Management

Fate seems to have taken a hand in directing Jack Gallagher toward his successful career in property management. Fresh out of the army and eager to further his education, Gallagher met a girl at a party who worked as a secretary in a real estate office. Soon they were married, and he was looking for a source of part-time income while he attended college.

Through his wife's employer, Gallagher became a night maintenance man in return for a free apartment in the building. One night, as he checked in with the property office, he found the on-site manager searching frantically for someone to clean a vacant apartment so that tenants could move in the next day. Gallagher took the job. Within a short time, he was operating his own cleaning service with several employees.

Two years later, Gallagher's business was a success, but he decided that real estate was really the field that interested him. He began as a resident manager for an 890-unit complex. One year later, to the day, he was fired.

Looking back on his early false start, Gallagher admits that he and his employer were not suited to each other. The company's style of management was very structured, while Gallagher's was more spontaneous and off the cuff.

Gallagher left the resident manager's job on Friday, and by Monday he had a position with Shannon and Luchs (now Polinger Shannon & Luchs Company), where he began working in the early 1980s. His first job was in the newly created condominium management department, and he quickly made a place for himself.

In the years that followed, Gallagher moved into commercial management, then back to the condominium department as its head, and then finally to his current position as vice president of all property management operations.

Regardless of what type of property he operated, Gallagher found many similarities. Whether it is a condominium or an office building, the manager still has to wash the floors and keep the heat going.

Gallagher found that the major difference occurred in tenant attitudes. In an apartment, tenants could become very emotional about problems, because an apartment represents most people's total belongings as well as their sense of home.

On the other hand, except for the owner and the office manager, most tenants in an office building aren't too concerned if there is a problem. "It is just a day off for them," he concludes.

Gallagher has seen major changes in the property management business since he first entered the field. He points particularly to the growth of corporate, pension fund, and foreign ownership of U.S. and Canadian real estate. This trend, in turn, has prompted more consolidation among real estate management companies. "The little guy is being squeezed out," he warns.

Yet Gallagher believes there is still great opportunity in property management for those with the knowledge of law, finance, and marketing demanded by today's sophisticated commercial property owners.

Outlook

The Bureau of Labor Statistics estimates that as of 2004, there were approximately 361,000 individuals engaged in property management. The bureau predicts that demand for property managers will increase at least as rapidly as national demand for all occupations through 2014. It estimates that the number of property managers will increase by 15.3 percent between 2004 and 2014, rising to 416,000 positions. Within the industry itself, the demand remains strong for managers with strong financial skills who can add value to investment real estate. Shortages of qualified higher-level executives is also contributing to annual increases in earnings of between 3.5 and 5.5 percent, according to a 2006 National Real Estate Earnings and Benefits Survey conducted by CEL & Associates. Note that this survey was not limited to property managers. Estimates by JobFutures.ca, a website of Service Canada, estimates that demand for property administrators will be better than average during the next few years.

There also are emerging management opportunities in a variety of areas that did not even exist a few years ago. Today, property managers are specializing in areas such as assisted-care housing, which offers support in daily living to an increasing elderly population. At another extreme, more schools and universities are turning to private management to fill their housing needs. Resort and second-home management is another growing area.

Whether it is managing rooftop sites for telecommunications equipment, military housing for U.S. troops, or fast-food outlets for a regional chain, every company that needs real estate—and that is virtually every company—needs the services of a talented real estate manager.

9

Asset and Portfolio Manager

The asset and portfolio manager is the highest level of property management, apart from the owner. Indeed, the job of the portfolio manager is to act in place of the owner, making decisions not only about how the property should be operated but also when it should be bought, renovated, or sold.

The portfolio manager is sometimes called an asset manager, because he or she is responsible for preserving the value of the asset (the property). However, the term *asset manager* is not clearly defined and is often applied to property managers and others who do not really have responsibility for an entire real estate portfolio. In large national real estate investment trusts (REITs) or real estate companies, a regional manager may perform many of the functions of an asset manager and assume that title. Corporations are also increasingly outsourcing much of their real estate function to companies that perform asset management.

Job Description

The portfolio or asset manager has responsibility for a large group of properties, often of more than one type. This group is referred to as a *portfolio of properties*, just as a group of different stocks is referred to as a *stock portfolio*. This portfolio is usually owned by a bank, a pension fund, a corporation, or a group of foreign investors. In some cases, the bank or pension fund represents the interest of many smaller owners who have joined together to own the property.

The manager must report to his or her owner company or, in the case of an REIT, to the company's board of directors and shareholders on the overall performance of the portfolio and must gain company approval for buying, selling, or major expenditures. However, the portfolio manager makes most of the decisions for the property and oversees the work of property managers to ensure that the company's plans are carried out.

The exact responsibilities of every portfolio or asset manager are different, but some tasks they perform include:

- Analyzing the financial requirements of each property and approving rental rates and budgets.
- Giving final approval of all leases. Portfolio managers may participate in lease negotiations for very large users.
- Identifying alternative sources of income for the property that might improve income. For example, the rooftops of taller buildings may be leased to cellular phone providers.
- Setting strategies for acquiring new properties and integrating them into the portfolio.
- Authorizing the implementation of management policies and procedures.

- Identifying and approving major renovations or expenditures.
- Supervising the work of property supervisors, either those working in-house or third-party managers.

Because he or she is usually responsible for the management of many properties, the portfolio or asset manager visits properties infrequently. Instead, he or she receives information on financial performance and leasing from the property supervisors. Some companies, including most REITs, employ property supervisors on staff and locate them at regional offices where they can oversee property operations. Others prefer to hire local fee management companies in the area of a property to manage it. Some companies combine the two approaches.

If property supervisors are employed by the company, the portfolio manager may have the responsibility of supervising their work. Here again, as with the executive property manager, this management often takes place long distance, so property supervisors must be competent to act on their own.

If the company employs third-party fee managers, the portfolio manager is often responsible for selecting the firms used. The manager will usually ask likely firms to submit proposals describing how they will manage the property, what they think the profit from the property will be, and what fees they will charge for this management. The manager then reviews proposals, talks with representatives of the management companies, and checks references, just as he or she would when buying any other service.

Another part of the portfolio manager's job is to decide whether the composition of the portfolio is appropriate for the conditions of the current real estate market and the owner's goals. For example, if after studying market trends the portfolio or asset manager believes that values of shopping centers in the Southeast will fall significantly, he or she may decide to sell some such properties from the portfolio. In this way, if economic conditions for one part of the country decline, the overall portfolio will not be too adversely affected.

Asset managers who work on behalf of corporations may also help determine how space can be used to meet a company's business goals and help to lease additional space when it is needed.

Education

Although there are no formal educational requirements for a portfolio or asset manager, it is unlikely that the major companies that hire them would accept anything less than a college degree, preferably with study in business and real estate. Many portfolio managers today have advanced degrees in business, finance, or real estate. M.B.A. degrees are also common within this group.

In general, most portfolio managers have experience in real estate, either in development, brokerage, or property management. In some instances, portfolio managers enter their positions from the fields of banking and finance. Portfolio managers also may be promoted from the ranks of property supervisors in companies that use in-house managers.

A strong financial background is particularly important for the portfolio manager, because he or she relies on financial reports for much of the information on the property. A portfolio manager should also have a good understanding of financial analysis and spreadsheet programs used for property reviews.

At the same time, knowledge of real estate and property operations is an essential component for the portfolio manager. Because real estate is a physical entity, not a piece of paper like a stock or bond, the portfolio manager must understand the fundamentals of property maintenance, renovation, and leasing. Often this experience is gained firsthand while working in some part of the real estate field.

Earnings

Because asset management covers a wide range of financial and tenant-relation responsibilities, asset managers—whether they work for banks, institutions, or REITs—often receive significant earnings for their efforts. Earnings usually include a base salary plus performance-based bonuses and often stock options.

A 2005 survey conducted by CEL & Associates found that the median salary for the top property management executive at an REIT or publicly traded real estate company was $233,400. The top asset manager at an REIT earned $238,200.

Another CEL & Associates survey revealed that top asset management executives working with office/industrial properties earned a median of $169,100. Top asset managers for multifamily portfolios earned $142,800, and for retail they earned $198,600.

A 2006 survey by FPL Associates L.P., a group of companies focused on providing corporate and managerial services to the real estate industry, determined that a senior asset management executive earned a median base salary of $125,760 and a median total reimbursement of $176,564. An associate asset manager or data analyst earned $65,750 in total compensation.

In the same FPL Associates L.P. survey, senior portfolio managers, who oversee a group of investment-grade assets, earned a median total compensation of $169,681. A mid-level portfolio manager earned a median of $116,708 in total remuneration.

These top individuals are responsible for the supervision and performance of a company-wide portfolio of assets. They formulate long-range plans for these assets and hold ultimate authority for all decisions that affect investment performance.

Profile of an Asset Manager

Like many property managers over the age of thirty, Reggie Mullins, senior portfolio manager for Cushman and Wakefield, "fell into property management." Today, most managers hold college degrees, but Mullins began her real estate career after one year of college as an administrative assistant for nine development project managers. Right across the aisle from her desk was the company's sole property manager.

"I was the type of person who asked questions, and when I asked, he told me about what the terms in the contracts and work orders meant." Soon Mullins was taking tenant phone calls and developing property budgets. When her boss discovered her skills, she was promoted to property manager.

Her boss also helped her up the ladder by sending her to training courses conducted by the Institute of Real Estate Management. She was scared at first. "I was in tears the first day of the course, thinking I couldn't do it," she recalls, "but my boss convinced me to go on, and I passed." With training, the networking contacts she's made in IREM, and that old curiosity, she now manages sixty people and three-million-plus square feet of property for major institutional clients. (She did go back and complete her degree in 2000 to demonstrate to her daughter the importance of education.)

Mullins says these days her job is more about "people and process than properties." Although accounting skills are critical, she says, she most enjoys the people aspects of property management,

"Helping others grow so you can do the same." She also enjoys the fact no day is ever the same as the day before.

The downside is that you're always on call. "These days, in the case of an emergency, I may be fifth on the list of people to call behind the engineer and the property manager, but I'm still on the list," she says.

Profile of an REIT Manager

Today, Alexandra (Alex) Jackiw may be a regional vice president of AIMCO, the largest single owner of apartment properties in the United States, but she got her start in property management because she couldn't find a job in her chosen field—social work.

She had managed housing for students as part of a graduate assistantship while attending the University of Ohio. She was able to translate that experience and her degree into a position with a government agency that helped poorer families with housing.

At first, Jackiw admits, she was more interested in the social aspects of the housing program than in the "bricks and sticks," but after working through several renovations, she found that she liked the opportunity the job gave her to influence peoples' lives in a positive way. For the next five years, Jackiw worked in several governmental agencies managing housing for the elderly and public housing for families. She got a good basic background in management and learned "to do a lot with a few resources." However, she found the red tape and slow decision making of government frustrating. "It was an exercise in patience," she says. When a political upheaval shook the housing authority, Jackiw was one of the many sacrificed to politics—she was fired.

In retrospect, she calls the forced change the best thing that ever happened to her. She initially had to take a step back and accept a position as an on-site manager for Oxford Development Company. "The position was an eye-opener. I lived on-site, and I gained a whole new perspective on what residents want and need," she said.

At Oxford, Jackiw again proved herself, becoming national director of training and marketing. She improved her presentation skills by teaching courses of the National Apartment Association and the Institute of Real Estate Management. Today, she still teaches and speaks at three or four conventions a year.

When Oxford was purchased by NHP Inc., Jackiw kept her training responsibilities and expanded her expertise to federally assisted housing. In 1997 NHP was acquired by AIMCO, one of the country's largest real estate investment trusts.

Working for a successful REIT has its own sets of challenges and rewards. At AIMCO, Jackiw was encouraged not to just be a pencil pusher but to get out into the field and supervise properties. She was able to see firsthand how a property was developed and what sort of work it took to reposition an investment successfully.

But the pressures on an REIT for quarterly performance can make life hectic. "Acquisitions come along fast and furious, and you are constantly running to keep pace," says Jackiw. The upside, she says, is that managers are expected and empowered to make decisions. "The buck stops here, but you have a real influence over where things are going."

Ultimately Jackiw likes property management because it's an exciting and creative business. It provides constant change and continuing opportunity for growth.

Outlook

There are still a relatively small number of jobs for portfolio managers compared to jobs for property supervisors. However, the tremendous growth in recent years in the amount of property owned by REITS, pension funds, and other institutions has increased the demand for asset managers. For example, the twenty-two hundred members of the Pension Real Estate Association—whose members oversee many corporate and state pension funds—each owned about $1.8 million in real estate in 2005, and more than two-thirds of members surveyed planned to increase their real estate holdings by 60 to 100 percent in the near future.

Because portfolio managers are high up on the property management ladder, individuals hoping to reach these positions must first gain experience at lower levels of real estate management. But as more development companies and national management firms build property management departments, it will become easier to advance to the level of portfolio manager within a structured company environment.

10

Property Manager as Business Owner

Like people in many other professions, property managers often dream of owning their own business—of being their own boss. Because most property management is still a locally based service business that can be started without a great deal of capital, owning a property management business is a feasible goal. In 2005 the Bureau of Labor Statistics estimated that more than one-half of all property, real estate, and community association managers were self-employed.

Opening a property management business is similar to opening any small service business. However, there are also specific concerns relating to the field of management.

Demand for Fee Management

Although the trend in the property management business is toward larger owners with their own management departments, most owners, large and small, still hire fee managers to operate their buildings. In a 2004 research study published by the Institute of Real Estate Management, 22.3 percent of all managers surveyed worked for firms with ten or fewer employees. In the same survey, almost 18 percent of those responding said that they were the owner or a partner in the company they worked for.

In another 2004 survey, IREM determined that the average management company that held its Accredited Management Organization (AMO) designation employed 240 people. Almost half of that number worked as property managers, assistant property managers, or on-site managers.

As the name implies, a fee manager supervises property for a fee. Depending on the nature of the management contract, the property manager may have all the responsibilities of the owner or may make only the routine decisions for the property.

The basis for defining the job of the fee property manager is the management agreement between the owner and the management company. The agreement will usually require the manager to hire workers and buy services for the property, to keep all financial records for the property and report them to the owner, and to oversee the leasing of the building. The management company also may be asked to supervise renovation of the property or handle other special projects.

The management company will then hire people to work on the building. The number of people that the management company assigns to each property depends upon the size of the building, how difficult the management job seems to be (for example, is the building empty or full), and the agreed-upon fee.

There are no set rules for what fee a management company can charge; however, 4 to 6 percent of revenues are standard. Usually the management company receives a set fee for operating the property as well as bonuses for signing leases or for lowering costs. Additional fees may be charged for special projects such as renovations.

In the 2004 survey of AMO firms, IREM determined that these companies earned approximately 80 percent of their income from management. Most of the remainder came from leasing commissions or commissions on property sales.

Starting a Business

Because of the high failure rate associated with starting a small business, personal determination and a strong business plan are a must before trying to open a property management firm.

Many people are attracted to the idea of operating a small business because they will be their own boss. While it is true that a small business owner is responsible for making all decisions for a company, always remember that the client is the real boss. If you do not satisfy an owner's expectations for his or her building, the business will not succeed.

Evaluating Your Character

A good first step in planning a small business is evaluating your own character as a business leader. The Small Business Administration website (www.sba.gov) suggests asking yourself the following questions:

- Am I a self-starter?
- How well do I get along with a variety of personalities?
- How good am I at making decisions?
- Do I have the emotional and physical stamina to run a business?
- How well do I plan and organize?
- Are my attitudes and drive strong enough to maintain motivation?
- How will the business affect my family?

Without the right attributes, succeeding with a small business may be difficult.

Financing Your Business

Another consideration in starting a small business is the money necessary to get the business going. Property management offers some advantages in this area, because unlike a retail or manufacturing business, it does not require a great deal of initial investment.

To estimate how much money you need to begin your management business, start by estimating all the expenses and potential income you can expect in the first six months of operation. Initial expenses include office rental, office furniture, salary for an assistant or answering service, marketing expenses for making owners aware of your property, taxes on income and Social Security payments, and money for you to live on during this period.

Next you must estimate potential income for the same period. Income will depend on the number of management contracts you can obtain. Keep in mind, however, that negotiating agreements with prospective owners may take some time, so do not overestimate your income. Market conditions in your area also will influence your income potential. The Small Business Administration provides excellent guidelines and worksheets to help you estimate income and costs for your proposed business.

Money for starting a small business may be obtained from banks, providing you have reasonable credit. A bank will expect to see a business plan with estimated costs and an outline of how you expect to generate and serve clients. Other sources of funds include family and friends. Taking a partner may be another way to obtain additional financing.

Locating Customers

If you are a successful manager for an existing management company, some of the owners of buildings you have managed may be willing to transfer their business to your company. However, be careful in soliciting this business so as not to act unethically toward your former employer. Contacting developers of newly constructed buildings in your area and researching city records to find new owners of existing buildings also are good ways to locate business. If you have a background in real estate sales, home owners who cannot sell their homes or who own investment property may be interested in having you manage their properties. Friends and colleagues also may suggest potential business leads.

In addition, consider either buying all or part of an existing management business. If this business is successful and has a good reputation, you may already have some properties under contract on your first day of operation. In buying an existing business, be sure that management contracts are not null and void if the business is sold.

A tremendous new force in locating new customers is the Internet. Increasingly, companies look to the Web for research on buying and hiring decisions. In addition, the Internet has become a first line of information transfer between prospects and owners and between clients and property managers. Today, most companies can convey information about both the company and available properties via the Internet. Many companies also use the Internet and private intranets to give clients instant access to data about a property. Some companies even use real-time video to monitor construction projects via the Internet. Today, developing a strong Web presence that combines promotion and useful data is vital to finding new customers and serving existing ones.

Knowing the Laws

A final concern for all businesses is being aware of laws that affect business operation. The federal and many state and local governments have laws that regulate business operation. The real estate license law in your state is one example. Federal laws in both the United States and Canada regulate such personnel practices as worker's earnings, Social Security, and health benefits. Fair housing laws in both countries govern leasing and selling practices for real estate and prohibit discrimination based on race, ethnicity, national origin, familial status, or handicap. State laws may extend these protections to other groups as well. Environmental statutes, such as those relating to lead paint in housing, may affect managers of buildings. As the owner of the management business, you may be held liable if these laws are violated.

Earnings

According to the 2004 IREM survey, earnings levels for those who act as owners, partners, officers, and directors of a business are higher than for those working as employees. The survey found that those acting as officers in a company received a salary of $139,671 per year, while those acting as an owner or partner had an average salary of $147,236 a year.

Profile of an Owner of a Real Estate Business

When asked to describe the skills needed to excel in property management, Saadat M. Keshavjee jokingly chose the Kipling quote, "If you can keep your head when all about you are losing it and blaming it on you. . . ." The ability to think on your feet, analyze situations rapidly, and retain a sense that every customer is special form the basis of Keshavjee's successful business philosophy.

Keshavjee began his career in another business that emphasizes customer service—hotel management. Born in Africa, his parents sent him to school in England to study hotel management at Bournemouth. Immigrating to Canada, Keshavjee found hotel management rewarding, but he eventually wanted a position that allowed for more regular hours. It was then that he considered real estate. Keshavjee had taken an interest test while in college, and results said he should be a property manager or a trustee. Now seemed to be the time. Keshavjee accepted a position with a Calgary developer and began managing new properties as they were being sold. He worked on all types of properties—medical buildings, industrial installations, housing. "It was a tremendous learning experience," he said.

Keshavjee's next learning opportunity was his discovery of the Certified Property Manager (CPM) designation. As he describes it, "I was negotiating a lease on behalf of my company, and the man representing the tenant said to me, 'You're a tough negotiator; you must be a CPM.' Well, I didn't even know what that was. But this man, who was a CPM himself, introduced me to the educational courses and networking options the designation offered."

After five years in development, Keshavjee made the commitment to management, working first as a freelance troubleshooter for a variety of clients. There was a recession in Calgary at that time, so rather than starting a new business, he specialized in short-term assignments and in turning around difficult properties.

When the market stabilized, Keshavjee founded Amherst Management, the company he still heads. The company specializes in an often-overlooked area of real estate—the management of single-family homes and smaller apartment properties. He recognized that there was a niche for this type of management and has been very successful with it. "We focus on middle-market apartments and are very selective in the properties we take," he says.

Today, Keshavjee still finds property management both rewarding and challenging. "There is never a dull moment," he says. His job requires him to respond to about 150 phone calls a day and deal with problems ranging from grass fertilizers to investment strategies. And although technical knowledge of all kinds is important, Keshavjee emphasizes people skills as the most important for management success. He reminds his employees that property management is a service business in which responsiveness, attention to detail, and value are paramount. "That is the key to success in property management," he says.

Outlook

Succeeding in a business of one's own is the dream of many Americans, and property management is a career in which that dream can be realized. Before attempting to start a property management business, the property manager should have sound experience in the field as well as some experience in business management. Having sufficient capital to keep the business operating and pay employees for several months until the business is profitable is also critical for success. One way to help ensure success is to find a type of property that is growing in your area and specialize in that market niche. Another alternative is to purchase a share in an already successful property management business.

11

CAREERS RELATED TO PROPERTY MANAGEMENT

BECAUSE OF THE limited entry requirements to work in the field of property management, individuals in almost any line of work can become a property manager. However, working in certain related fields will help you learn about the field of property management.

Real Estate Sales

Many property managers began their careers in real estate sales, either residential or commercial. These salespeople may have become interested in property management because their company had a property management division. Indeed, some of those who work as property managers continue to sell property.

In some cases, brokers may become involved in property management by accident when they take over temporary management of a property that is slow to sell. In slow residential sales markets, real estate brokerage firms often rent and oversee single-family homes for owners who have moved to a new home but have been unable to sell their former one. These agents and brokers find that fees for managing property provide a solid income base compared to the more erratic income from real estate sales. In addition, an owner interested in selling a building may turn first to the property manager he or she knows as a source of sales leads. Many property managers believe that property management and sales complement each other.

Responsibilities

Real estate salespeople are hired by real estate owners to find buyers for their properties. Sometimes, a buyer will hire a salesperson to help locate a property to buy. Most real estate salespeople work primarily with residential properties, although an estimated 10 percent of those in the field specialize in commercial, industrial, or special-use properties. Salespeople may work for a brokerage firm or start their own firms if they meet certain licensing requirements. The National Association of REALTORS (NAR), the major trade organization for residential real estate sales, estimates that in 2005 there were approximately eighty-five hundred to nine thousand residential real estate brokerage offices in the United States.

Using such sources as past buyers, new arrivals in the community, and referrals from friends and past customers, the salesperson contacts possible buyers and shows them available properties. These properties may be listed—that is, placed up for sale—directly with a salesperson's firm. Persuading sellers to list their properties with his or her firm is another part of the real estate salesperson's job.

Salespeople must often show property to prospective buyers on weekends and evenings, so the salesperson seldom works a regular nine-to-five schedule. Salespeople must also travel from one property to another with buyers.

Education

Real estate salespeople may already have some of the knowledge needed to move into the area of real estate management. All real estate brokers and sales agents must hold a real estate license, and most states require that licensees complete some form of education before taking the licensing examination. Many states also require regular continuing education to retain a real estate license. Salespeople will have some knowledge of real estate finance and business acquired while closing sales and explaining the costs of ownership to prospective buyers. Commercial brokers will also be able to read and understand building financial statements as part of their sales efforts.

Real estate agents and brokers will have already gained some selling skills that could be applied to leasing space. They will have learned about market conditions in their areas, which will be valuable in leasing and promoting rental properties. For example, they may know that buyers in their area repeatedly ask for houses with microwave ovens and suggest this amenity to a property owner as a way to lease apartments.

The *2005 National Association of REALTORS Member Profile* found that 46 percent of its members had earned a bachelor's degree or higher. A 2006 survey of NAR commercial members revealed that 69 percent held at least a bachelor's degree.

Earnings

Most salespeople rely on commissions from their sales as their only source of income. These commissions are based on a percentage of the sale price of a property and usually are paid only when the property changes hands. If a sale falls through, the salesperson receives nothing. In some instances, brokerage firms pay salespeople a regular monthly amount, which is then charged against their commission.

According to the 2005 member profile conducted by the National Association of REALTORS, the average residential salesperson belonging to NAR earned a median income of $49,300 in annual compensation. The U.S. Bureau of Labor Statistics determined that real estate agents and brokers working in real estate offices earned a median income of $37,970 in 2004. In general, the earnings of real estate salespeople are lower than those of property managers.

Service Canada estimates that average earnings for real estate agents and salespeople in the Toronto area were $30.30 (Canadian dollars) per hour in 2000. The agency's website, www.labourmar ketinformation.ca, has estimates for earnings in most provinces.

Of course, the successful salesperson may easily earn more than the average property manager. On the other hand, a real estate salesperson's earnings are often totally dependent on what he or she sells. Consequently, income may be very erratic, with a big commission one month and then no income the next. Because the property manager's income is still based on a salary, earnings are more stable. Of course, the successful manager may also earn commissions on leasing.

The property manager is also more likely to receive company benefits, such as hospitalization and paid vacation, than is the salesperson. Many real estate salespeople work as independent contractors, and this means they receive few employee benefits and must provide their own. These extras add value to the property manager's earnings. The Bureau of Labor Statistics estimates that the demand for real estate brokers and agents will increase by 24 percent between 2004 and 2014.

Jobfutures.ca, a website of Services Canada, estimates that demand for real estate agents will be average, with jobs opening up as older workers retire. However, the site notes that real estate sales—unlike property management—are cyclical, and jobs will increase or decrease depending on the health of real estate construction activity.

Property Maintenance and Systems Administration

One way that many individuals have entered the property management profession is through maintenance work at a property. Although increasing sophistication in the management field makes this route more difficult than it has been in the past, there are still opportunities for advancement.

Although many properties contract with outside suppliers for such services as cleaning and landscaping, almost every sizable property employs at least some maintenance personnel. The size of the staff may vary from one part-time maintenance worker at a small apartment building to a multiperson staff at a major shopping center. Larger properties may employ maintenance supervisors who coordinate staff and purchasing in the maintenance, groundskeeping, and janitorial areas. Workers in all of these positions are well suited to gain firsthand knowledge of property operations.

Responsibilities

Maintenance personnel at a property perform a variety of scheduled and emergency duties. Maintenance workers assist residents with minor electrical and plumbing problems. They change light bulbs in offices, stores, and apartment common areas. They repaint units, repair broken signs, and fix holes in parking lots. They clean gutters and swimming pools, caulk windows, replace locks, repair appliances, and perform routine service on heating equipment.

The increasing sophistication of heating and security systems in office buildings makes it less likely that on-site staff can handle such repairs. However, the maintenance staff in a commercial building has to be comfortable enough with technology to monitor building performance using sophisticated computerized systems. Another part of the maintenance worker's schedule is based on an annual maintenance plan drawn up by the on-site manager or the maintenance supervisor. These routine tasks involve regular servicing of equipment, cleaning, and replacement of worn components.

Yet another portion of the maintenance job is responding to emergency repair requests from tenants. These emergencies may range from a stopped-up sink to a burst plumbing line that is flooding a store. While most properties call in specialists for major repair work, the property's maintenance staff is first on the spot. To respond to tenant emergencies, members of a maintenance staff are often on call day and night.

The maintenance staff also provides an important area of contact with tenants. A pleasant, rapid response to a problem creates tremendous tenant goodwill. Thus, good communication skills are an important part of the maintenance worker's abilities.

Today's more sophisticated building technologies have created a new level of professionalism for maintenance workers. For example, the Building Owners and Managers International Association offers designations for both systems administrators and systems technicians. These posts, which are usually associated with either a larger property or with oversight of several properties near each other, require skills in energy management, electrical systems, and air-handling systems, among other skills.

In addition to the standard maintenance duties, properties that have a maintenance supervisor may want employees able to oversee and train workers, make purchases, and work with the property supervisor to plan routine maintenance work. In cases where building security is provided by an in-house staff, the maintenance supervisor may also oversee those activities.

The U.S. Bureau of Labor Statistics estimates that the demand for building maintenance workers will rise by almost 22 percent between 2004 and 2014.

Education

Most maintenance workers learn their skills on the job or as apprentices in a trade, such as carpentry or plumbing. Few formal training courses are available, although the Building Owners and Managers Association does offer a course in property maintenance leading to the designation. Trade associations in specific maintenance skills also offer specialized training.

The exposure to the physical operation of a property that the maintenance worker gains is valuable to the on-site manager or property supervisor in establishing budgets and in overseeing property performance. Similarly, the familiarity with tenant relations is also a good skill for those eager to move into management.

In most cases, the maintenance worker would have to acquire additional education in real estate before moving up to the field of property management. Some maintenance workers may be promoted to the job of on-site manager, but it is probably difficult to move beyond this point without further training.

Earnings

According to a survey published in the July 2004 issue of *Managing Housing Letter*, median annual earnings for a maintenance supervisor are $29,725. However, a 2005 earnings study by CEL & Associates placed the median for maintenance supervisor salaries at $58,400. The same survey found that maintenance engineers earned a median salary of $38,300.

The *Managing Housing Letter* survey determined that janitorial workers and porters at commercial properties earned a median of $20,000 in 2004. In the same year, the U.S. Bureau of Labor Statistics found that maintenance workers involved with real estate activities had a median hourly wage of $12.71. A 2006 survey by the Building Owners and Managers Association Canada found that chief office building engineers earned $50,000 to $70,000 (Canadian dollars) annually. Maintenance workers in the same survey earned $30,000 to $60,000.

Clerical Work

Individuals who hold clerical positions in property management offices are often in an excellent position to learn about the skills required to manage property successfully.

Responsibilities

Clerical workers, sometimes called *office administrators*, employed at individual properties or at a central property management office work regularly with a variety of property information. Office workers at a property may accept rent payments and keep track of lease expirations and changes using property management or accounting software programs. They may order materials and monitor payment of bills to suppliers. In the absence of the on-site manager, a clerical worker also may have to handle tenant complaints or emergencies. All of these responsibilities help give the clerical worker a good overall understanding of the property manager's job.

A clerical worker at a central property management office probably has less direct tenant contact but works more with financial information and budgeting. Often clerical workers help property supervisors gather information to create property budgets and compile financial statements for owners. Clerical workers also may assist in doing market research on a property.

Education

Clerical workers in a property management office should possess the same general office skills as for any other office job. In addition, because many management offices have few employees, the office worker may be required to perform a wide variety of duties.

A background with courses in accounting or finance will be especially helpful in compiling and ordering property budget information. Training in computer use is also vital, as virtually all managers keep property records on the computer. The clerical worker who hopes to move up in the field of property management should focus on real estate and business courses.

Earnings

According to the survey in the July 2004 issue of *Managing Housing Letter*, clerical workers at property management firms earned a median annual salary of $19,000. Reported salaries ranged from $14,712 to $22,750. Salaries for clerical workers in property management are not comparable to higher level clerical workers. According to the *Occupational Outlook Handbook, 2006–2007,* secretaries and administrative assistants had salaries of $34,970 in 2004. In most cases, clerical workers at management companies receive the same benefits as clerical workers in other types of companies.

The U.S. Bureau of Labor Statistics projects that demand for general administrative staff will rise slightly more than 27 percent between 2004 and 2014.

Other Fields

Almost any field connected with finance, law, or real estate serves as a good gateway to work in property management. Experience in some form of sales also may be useful. A background in finance is often found among those moving into positions with larger institutional owners and is probably essential for those hoping to move up to the position of property manager.

Because there are few specific requirements to enter the property management business, the field still offers opportunities for those seeking a new, growing career. To others, the field offers the chance for individual business ownership and rewards tied closely to actual performance. There is no one sure path to a career in property management. However, for many workers, young and old, the field of property management offers an exciting challenge.

12

FUTURE OF PROPERTY MANAGEMENT

IN THE YEARS ahead, the field of property management will be filled with opportunities for both beginners and established managers. The U.S. Department of Labor's Bureau of Labor Statistics estimates that approximately 361,000 people worked in property management in 2004. The Bureau of Labor Statistics predicts that employment of property managers will increase at least as fast as the average for all jobs through 2014. There will always be buildings to manage and owners who care about the value of their properties. Increasingly, owners and tenants alike are recognizing that well-educated, dedicated managers make the difference between an adequate property and an excellent one.

However, in the years ahead, property management also will become a much more sophisticated business than it is today. Several trends are contributing to this increased professionalism:

- Securitization and globalization of real estate ownership
- Impact of technology and the Internet on real estate marketing, operations, and transactions
- Greening of commercial real estate
- Demographic shifts resulting from offshoring and telecommuting

Each of these factors will place demands on the property manager of the twenty-first century, and only those capable of meeting those challenges will succeed.

Securitization of Real Estate

For most of its existence, real estate and the real estate industry have been local. Land did not move, and those who knew it best were those who lived near it. However, real estate today is increasingly dependent on national and international flows of capital to provide funds to develop and purchase property. Banks and insurance companies were once the primary, private sources of real estate lending. Today, the loans that real estate professionals need for building or rehabbing and the money spent by pension funds and other institutional investors to purchase properties compete with loans for computer chip plants in Korea and auto plants in India. Recent market fluctuations have shown that the prosperity of real estate is closely linked to world conditions.

The growth of real estate investment trusts (REITs) and other publicly traded securities that sell on stock exchanges, as well as the creation of large regional and national firms, has produced some fundamental changes in the way real estate management is done.

The need to perform on a quarterly basis for Wall Street analysts has increased the importance of management significantly at the same time that it has increased pressure to find new sources of revenue. If Wall Street has given real estate a place among global industries, it also has shown that to attract capital, real estate must operate in a new way.

Today, managers for REITs and public companies must possess financial and investment skills that were unknown in the industry a decade ago. At the same time, the consolidations and mergers of recent years have undercut job security and compelled many managers to do more with less. The consolidation of diverse companies through mergers has also brought its own challenges. Skills in working with employees of different backgrounds and in forging alliances with ever-changing partners will be of high value in the decades ahead.

The creation of larger companies also creates new opportunities for those in property management. Large companies enable employees to grow within the organization and can offer more possible career paths. Generally speaking, larger companies have more to spend on education and can offer more training to help employees excel. On the personal side, public companies often offer valuable stock options to employees and usually can provide better benefits because of their larger size.

Although there will almost certainly be room for smaller management companies in the future, the trend toward larger, public companies will continue to grow. In the twenty-first century, real estate managers are just as likely to work for an REIT or public real estate company as for a small local firm. Each has its benefits and drawbacks, and astute managers will choose which is best for them.

Technology and Property Management

As is the case with all business today, recent advances in technology have had a tremendous impact on the real estate management business. Today's residents use websites, complete with virtual tours, to view apartments and learn more about the neighborhoods they are located in. Once residents move in, wired apartments offer community newsletters via e-mail, property and community blogs, closed-circuit TV security, and on-site business centers with T-1 lines. Some management companies even allow residents to pay their rent online. Office users rely on the Internet to view floor plans, exchange lease negotiations, and watch real-time construction via closed-circuit digital cameras. Although commercial real estate still lacks a comprehensive nationally recognized Internet listing that is present in residential sales, the industry is increasingly working toward the wider distribution of listings. Shopping centers continue to hold their own against e-commerce with more entertainment and their own versions of virtual shopping. However, continued consolidation of retailers makes it more of a challenge to find and keep tenants.

In business, companies use intranets to communicate orders to vendors and to make property information available at any time to owners. Individual properties transfer leasing data and rent collections via modem. Even training is increasingly conducted via CD or online. The easy availability of data over the Internet has also made it easier for smaller property management firms to compete with larger companies. Once only the biggest companies could support research departments; today individual managers can access data rapidly and affordably.

Property managers also use the Web to attract clients, with 85 percent of respondents using a company site to attract business, according to a 2004 survey conducted by the Institute of Real Estate Management.

Computerization of property management operations is not the only technology influencing managers in the years ahead. Sophisticated building systems to control heat and light and to provide security are becoming widespread. Although the manager will not need to operate such systems directly, the property and on-site managers will be charged with training personnel to run these systems.

The property manager also is increasingly responsible for offering tenants a variety of telecommunications options at the property. Residential managers must negotiate with providers of cable TV, satellite, telephone, and high-speed Internet access to keep residents happy. Office managers must negotiate between Wi-Fi and satellite providers to ensure that tenants can meet their telecom needs without filling the building with miles of unneeded cabling. Revenues must be negotiated for rooftop space leased to cell phone, pager, and other communications providers. Increased government regulation makes it still harder for managers to remain current in this important area.

A 2004 survey of building technologies conducted by the Institute of Real Estate Management found that 56 percent of the buildings managed by respondents had high-speed Internet access and 28 percent were wired for broadband. Other common technology systems found in buildings included automated fire and safety controls (54 percent) and automated lighting controls (50 percent).

Greening of Commercial Real Estate

Higher energy prices as well as concerns for the environment among employers and workers are also leading to more emphasis on environmentally sensitive building construction and operation. As of 2005 more than six thousand commercial buildings had been certified as meeting the Leadership in Energy and Environmental Design (LEEDS) standards developed by the U.S. Green Buildings Council. While the idea of "green" office buildings is not new, many experts believe that it has reached a point of widespread adoption.

Green building operations require a wide set of skills, including knowledge of how to reduce energy costs from heating and lighting without sacrificing tenant comforts. Green buildings also incorporate features ranging from low-flow toilets that reduce water use to bike racks and showers that encourage workers to cycle to their jobs. Landscaping is also part of the green equation, as buildings emphasize plants that require less water. Managers must also be conscious of energy-saving products when selecting materials for cleaning, for renovation, or for installing amenities for tenants.

Managers will take on the role of green trainer by teaching and encouraging tenants to conserve energy by turning off lights and participating in recycling programs.

Offshoring and Telecommuting

Two factors that may influence demand for office space are the shift of more office jobs overseas and the increasing ability of workers to perform their work outside of the office. In 2004, Forrester Research, a Cambridge, Massachusetts, company, estimated that more than 3.3 million office jobs will move to other countries such as China and Russia over the next fifteen years. The company predicted that this job migration would reduce the demand for office space by six hundred million square feet.

The power of the Internet and mobile electronic devices has made it much more feasible for many workers to complete their jobs outside of a traditional office. From accountants to salespeople to customer service representatives, more companies are reducing their real estate costs by letting workers operate from home. This reduced need for space is also allowing companies to reduce the amount of space per worker, which also contributes to the reduced need for space.

Although it is difficult to say to what degree companies will move jobs or expand their telecommuting, vacant office space will negatively affect the demand for managers. At the same time, higher vacancies may create more demand for those managers with leasing skills.

The Future Is Bright

As the field of property management becomes more sophisticated, it remains one of almost unlimited opportunity. For those with drive, interest in solving problems, and a love of people, the property management area remains a very attractive career choice.

Appendix A

Schools Offering Real Estate Majors

Compiling a list of schools offering courses in property management is an almost impossible task. The following list of schools that offer bachelor's or master's degrees (associate degrees are not included) was compiled in part from *Peterson's Four-Year Colleges*, 2006 edition. However, many colleges and some privately owned real estate schools may teach one or more courses in property management. Other universities may have graduate-level programs in real estate. Local chapters of some of the national associations listed in Appendix B also offer real estate courses periodically. Check schools in your area for specific courses.

Arizona

Arizona State University

British Columbia

Langara College
University of British Columbia

California

California State Polytechnic University
California State University–Dominguez Hills
California State University–East Bay
California State University–Fresno
California State University–Sacramento
San Diego State University
San Francisco State University
University of Southern California

Colorado

Colorado State University
University of Colorado–Boulder
University of Denver

Connecticut

University of Connecticut
University of Hartford

District of Columbia

American University–Washington
George Washington University

Florida

Florida Atlantic University
Florida International University
Florida State University

University of Florida
University of Miami

Georgia

Georgia State University
University of Georgia
University of West Georgia

Hawaii

University of Hawaii–Manoa

Illinois

DePaul University
Northwestern University

Indiana

Ball State University
Indiana University–Bloomington

Iowa

University of Northern Iowa

Kentucky

Eastern Kentucky University
Morehead State University

Maryland

Johns Hopkins University

Massachusetts

Massachusetts Institute of Technology

Michigan

Marquette University

Minnesota

Minnesota State University–Mankato
St. Cloud State University
University of St. Thomas

Mississippi

Mississippi State University
University of Mississippi

Missouri

University of Missouri–Columbia
Webster University

Nebraska

University of Nebraska–Omaha

Nevada

University of Nevada–Las Vegas

New Jersey

Rutgers University
Thomas Edison State College

New York

Cornell University
New York University
St. John's University

North Carolina

St. Augustine's College
University of North Carolina

Ohio

The Ohio State University
University of Cincinnati
University of Toledo

Oklahoma

University of Central Oklahoma

Ontario

University of Guelph
University of Waterloo

Pennsylvania

Clarion University of Pennsylvania
Lehigh University
Peirce College
Temple University
University of Pennsylvania

South Carolina

Clemson University
University of South Carolina

Tennessee

The University of Memphis

Texas

Angelo State University
Baylor University
Southern Methodist University
Texas A&M University–Kingsville
Texas Christian University
University of Houston–Downtown
University of North Texas
University of Texas at Arlington
University of Texas at El Paso

Utah

Brigham Young University

Virginia

Virginia Tech University

Washington

Washington State University

Wisconsin

University of Wisconsin–Madison
University of Wisconsin–Milwaukee

Appendix B

Associations

ALTHOUGH THIS LIST does not attempt to cover every source related to real estate management, it will provide a good beginning for learning more about this diverse field.

American Real Estate and Urban Economics Association
P.O. Box 9958
Richmond, VA 23228
www.areuea.org

American Resort Development Association
1201 15th St. NW
Washington, DC 20005
www.arda.org

Building Owners and Managers Association, Canada
440 Laurier Ave. West, Ste. 200
Ottawa, ON K1R 7X6
www.bomacanada.ca

Building Owners and Managers Association International
1201 New York Ave. NW
Washington, DC 20005
www.boma.org

Building Owners and Managers Institute International
1521 Ritchie Hwy.
Arnold, MD 21012
www.bomi-edu.org

Canadian Real Estate Association
344 Slater St., Ste. 1600
Ottawa, ON K1R 7Y3
www.crea.org

CCIM Institute
430 N. Michigan Ave.
Chicago, IL 60611
www.ccim.com

Community Associations Institute
225 Reinekers La.
Alexandria, VA 22314
www.caionline.org

CoreNetGlobal
260 Peachtree St., Ste. 1500
Atlanta, GA 30303
www2.corenetglobal.org

Institute of Real Estate Management
430 N. Michigan Ave.
Chicago, IL 60611
www.irem.org

International Council of Shopping Centers
1221 Avenue of the Americas
New York, NY 10021
www.icsc.org

International Facility Management Association
1 E. Greenway Plaza
Houston, TX 77046
www.ifma.org

National Apartment Association
201 N. Union St.
Alexandria, VA 22314
www.naahq.org

National Association of Home Builders
1201 15th St. NW
Washington, DC 20005
www.nahb.com

National Association of Housing Cooperatives
1444 Eye St. NW, Ste. 700
Washington, DC 20005
www.coophousing.org

National Association of Industrial and Office Parks
2201 Cooperative Way
Herndon, VA 20171
www.naiop.org

National Association of Real Estate Investment Trusts
1875 I St. NW
Washington, DC 20006
www.nareit.org

National Association of REALTORS
430 N. Michigan Ave.
Chicago, IL 60611
www.realtor.org

National Association of Residential Property Managers
184 Business Park Dr.
Virginia Beach, VA 23462
www.narpm.org

National Multi Housing Council
1850 M St. NW
Washington, DC 20036
www.nmhc.org

National Property Management Association
28100 U.S. Hwy. 19 North, Ste. 400
Clearwater, FL 33761
www.npma.org

Real Estate Institute of Canada
5407 Eglinton Ave. West
Toronto, ON M9C 5K6
www.reic.ca

Real Property Association of Canada
1 University Ave, Ste. 1410
Toronto, ON M5J 2P1
www.realpac.ca

Urban Land Institute
1025 Thomas Jefferson
Washington, DC 20007
www.uli.org

Additional Resources

While there are many books, magazines, and websites about real estate and quite a few about property management, the following list may help you reach a better understanding of the property management business.

Books

Beirne, Mike. *Property Management Toolkit.* AMACOM, 2006.
Curren, Robert. *Apartment Property Management.* LuLu Press, 2004.
Ellison, Louise and Victoria Edwards. *Corporate Property Management.* Blackwell Publishing, 2003.
Griswold, Robert S. *Property Management for Dummies.* Wiley, 2001.
Institute of Real Estate Management. *Glossary of Real Estate Management Terms.* IREM, 2003.

Institute of Real Estate Management. *Principles of Real Estate Management*, 15th ed. IREM, 2006.

Kelley, Edward. *Practical Apartment Management*, 5th ed. IREM, 2004.

Kyle, Robert, Floyd Baird, and Marie Sodek. *Property Management*, 7th ed. Dearborn Real Estate Education, 2004.

Muhlebach, Richard F. and Alan A. Alexander. *Business Strategies for Real Estate Management Companies*, 2nd ed. IREM, 2004.

Patellis, Mike, David Kuperberg, and Barbara Dershowitz. *Residential Property Management*. National Association of Home Builders, 2003.

Portman, Janet. *Every Landlord's Guide to Finding Great Tenants*. Nolo, 2006.

Ross, Stan, with James Carberry. *The Inside Track to Careers in Real Estate*. Urban Land Institute, 2005.

Stewart, Marcia, Janet Portman, and Ralph Warner. *Every Landlord's Legal Guide*, 8th ed. Nolo, 2006.

Taylor, Jeffrey. *The Landlord's Kit*. Kaplan Business, 2002.

Teicholz, Eric. *Facilities Design and Management*. McGraw-Hill, 2001.

Weiss, Mark B. and Dan Baldwin. *Streetwise Landlording and Property Management*. Adams Media Corp., 2003.

Periodicals

This list does not include specific articles but rather some periodicals about real estate and property management.

Apartment Finance Today
Hanley-Wood LLC
Washington, DC

The BOMA Magazine
Building Owners and Managers Association
Washington, DC

Building Operating Management
Trade Press Publishing Corp.
Milwaukee, WI

Buildings
Stamats Communications
Des Moines, IA

Commercial Investment Real Estate
CCIM Institute
Chicago, IL

Commercial Property News
VNU Real Estate and Design Network
New York, NY

Common Ground
Community Associations Institute
Alexandria, VA

Development Magazine
National Association of Office and Industrial Parks
Arlington, VA

Facilities Design and Management
VNU Real Estate and Design Network
New York, NY

Journal of Property Management
Institute of Real Estate Management
Chicago, IL

Landlord Law Report
CD Publications
Silver Spring, MD

Managing Housing Letter
CD Publications
Silver Spring, MD

Multi-Family Executive
Hanley-Wood LLC
Washington, DC

Multi Housing News
VNU Real Estate and Design Network
New York, NY

National Real Estate Investor
Primedia, Inc.
Atlanta, GA

The RCA Report
REALTORS Commercial Alliance
National Association of REALTORS
Chicago, IL

Real Estate Forum
Real Estate Media
New York, NY

REALTOR Magazine
National Association of REALTORS
Chicago, IL

Retail Trade
Primedia, Inc.
Atlanta, GA

Shopping Centers Today
International Council of Shopping Centers
New York, NY

Units
National Apartment Association
Alexandria, VA

Urban Land
The Urban Land Institute
Washington, DC

Useful Websites

www.globest.com
(an industry news site)

www.inmannews.com
(industry news, primarily residential)

www.ired.com
(primarily focused on brokerage, but covers all aspects of the
   business)

Data Sites

The Small Business Administration
www.sba.gov

Canadian population figures
www.statcan.ca

Canadian industry statistics
www.strategis.ic.gc.ca

Commercial statistics
www.twr.com

Leasing Sites

www.costar.com

www.icx.ca

www.loopnet.com

www.move.com/apartments

About the Author

Mariwyn Evans graduated from Vanderbilt University in Nashville, Tennessee. She has written and edited several books on real estate, including *Modern Real Estate Practice, Virginia and Alabama Supplements for Modern Real Estate Practice, How About a Career in Real Estate?*, and *Opportunities in Real Estate Careers*, as well as *Profits from Real Estate Publicity*, done in conjunction with Howard S. Bimson. She has also helped to develop manuals used in teaching real estate principles and practices and real estate finance. She is currently communications manager for the REALTORS Commercial Alliance of the National Association of REALTORS. For twenty years she was editor of the *Journal of Property Management*, the official publication of the Institute of Real Estate Management in Chicago, Illinois.